EASY
INDIAN
COOKBOOK

EASY
INDIAN
COOKBOOK

THE STEP-BY-STEP GUIDE TO DELICIOUSLY EASY INDIAN FOOD AT HOME

MANJU MALHI

METRO BOOKS
NEW YORK

Managing Editor: Grace Cheetham
Editors: Beverly Le Blanc and Nicole Bator
Managing Designer: Manisha Patel
Designers: Luana Gobbo and Saskia Janssen
Studio Photography: William Lingwood
Photography Assistant: Kate Malone
Stylists: Jennifer White (food) and Helen Trent (props)

Metro Books
122 Fifth Avenue
New York, NY 10011

ISBN: 978-1-4351-2120-1

Printed and bound in Singapore

10 9 8 7 6 5 4 3 2 1

Author's acknowledgments

A big thank you to my mum Kami, Meno Malhi, Khazina, Werner Van
Peppen, Pauline Barrett, Robin Barrett, Jo and Nicholas Barrett, Louise
Robins, Juliana Barclay, Aruna Sood, Abha and Bill Adams, Sean Adams,
Girja Shanker Vohra, Monica Narula, Jeni Barnett, Alan Coxon, Paul
Hollywood, John Humphrys, Antony Worrall Thompson, Sonu Verma,
Sunita Verma, Puneet Gautam, Akshay Choubey, Seema Chandra, James
Macconachie, Stephanie Gerra, Rob Butler, Sam West, Robbie Sims, Matt
Barnard, James Shovlin, Tim Hughes, Laura Bootham, Nicola Phoenix,
Sudha Kaviraj, Neely Sood, Nik Gulhane, Matt and Kelly Brito, Leona
Daly, Simon Wain, Natasha Page, Liam Hamilton, Sophie Hillwood-Harris,
Caroline Blackadder, Dave Baker, Ben Robinson, Chris Kirby, Sanjay
Austa, Sona Sareen, Ceramica Blue, and Books for Cooks.

Publisher's note

Notes on the recipes

Unless otherwise stated:
• Use fresh herbs and chilies
• 1 tsp = 5ml
  1 tbsp = 15ml
  1 cup = 225ml

CONTENTS

INTRODUCTION

It's little wonder we are drawn to the cuisine of India: everything about it awakens the senses—sensuous aromas, vibrant colors, and fabulous textures are present in every element, from the smoothest, palest grain of rice to the intense crimson of delicate saffron threads. Indian cuisine is perfume for the nose, relish for the lips, nourishment for the body, and nectar for the soul.

India's one billion people eat what is naturally and seasonally available. Influenced by geography and climate, many religions and languages, and centuries of history, the country's 31 states boast a dizzying array of cuisines and specialties reflective of each region's character. In North India, the food is rich, with plenty of cream and warming spices to protect against the severe winters. In the extreme heat of the south, some of India's hottest and most exotic dishes feature fresh or green spices, which help to cool the body. Western India has embraced the most diverse and cosmopolitan global food trends, while to the east, where the Bengali and Assamese styles of cuisine are most prevalent, simplicity is key.

Given such diversity, it is ironic that when the rest of the world thinks of Indian food, curry is the first thing that springs to mind. In fact, although what we call curry is now recognized internationally, the term—originally coined by the British to describe the thousands of different stews and soups that shared common ingredients, such as turmeric, cumin, ginger, and chilies—is rarely used in India.

What unifies the cooking of this vast country, first and foremost, is not the use of "curry powder," as many believe, but rather a reliance on many spices and the ability to draw out and balance all of their distinctive flavors and aromas. Indian cooks are adept at concocting their own spice blends to season savory dishes. *Garam masala,* for example, which literally means a mixture of hot spices, is the most common, and every household will have its own special, signature combination. Chilies also appear frequently, but it is a common misconception that all Indian food is hot. Once you understand that the heat of a dish depends solely upon on the amount of chili it contains, you can easily adjust the intensity of a dish to suit your palette.

Dishes develop and change as a result of many factors. In India, certain foods are reserved for special occasions or festivals; others are taboo in some situations. Religion plays its part as well: Muslims do not eat pork because the pig is deemed unhygienic, and Hindus do not consume beef because the cow is considered sacred. The Hindu vegetarian tradition is widespread in India, yet many Hindus do eat meat. Furthermore, many of the dishes we think of as traditionally Indian actually sprang to life in the West. Chicken Tikka Masala (see page 84), for example, is one of the most popular curries outside India—but it was invented in British kitchens by Bangladeshi restaurateurs.

This book balances all of these influences, contrasts, and contradictions with the many similarities that characterize and unify Indian cooking. With recipes from every part of the country, along with some of the most popular restaurant inventions from the West, it is your guide to exploring, demystifying, and creating delicious, mouthwatering Indian meals you'll be proud to share with your friends and family.

PART 1

THE BASICS

Food without **spices** is like summer without sunshine—and this is very much the ethos of Indian **cooking**. First-time cooks often find the number of spices and ingredients used in Indian cuisine to be daunting—but the **simple** truth is that preparing an Indian meal is very **straightforward**. Mastering just a few basic techniques and becoming familiar with some of the **essential** ingredients will strip away the **mystery** and make preparing Indian food less time-consuming, much more satisfying, and incredibly **rewarding**.

Discover how to make **delicious** chutneys, relishes, and pickles to add layers of flavor to your **homecooked** meals. Move on to cooking with spices—by far the most important skill in Indian cooking. Begin by dry-roasting and **frying** spices, then **creating** flavorful spice blends. Breadmaking may be considered an art form by some, but with a little practice you'll be **surprised** at how easy Indian **breads**, such as naans and chapatis, are to make. Finally, learn the basic methods for preparing **traditional** Indian rice dishes, from Plain Basmati Rice to Saffron Rice and Tamarind Rice. Once you **master** the recipes in this chapter, you'll be on your way to opening a whole new world of Indian delights the **authentic** way.

INGREDIENTS

DAIRY

Clarified butter (ghee)—*Ghee* is clarified and evaporated butter made from cow or buffalo milk. Butter is melted and then simmered long enough to boil off all the water, during which time it develops a nutty taste. Although not a real substitute, normal butter comes close. However, ghee is available in most Asian food stores.

Paneer (paneer)—The most common Indian cheese, paneer, unlike most cheeses, does not melt when cooked, and it does not contain salt. It is an important source of protein for vegetarians and is used in both sweet and savory dishes.

Yogurt (dahi)—An essential ingredient in Indian cooking, yogurt is a staple for many vegetarians, and many homes in India still make their own practically every day. There are countless uses for yogurt, but the main ones are making yogurt drinks and chutneys, such as raitas, and using yogurt as a souring agent, a thickening agent, a meat tenderizer, and a flavor enhancer. The yogurt in India comes from buffalo milk and is thick and rich. Unsweetened, thick plain yogurt is the nearest substitute.

FRUIT AND VEGETABLES

Coconut (nariyal)—One of the most important ingredients in southern, western, and eastern vegetarian cooking is coconut. It is sliced, grated, or used in liquid form.

To prepare fresh coconut, place it over the kitchen sink and, using a hammer, pierce the soft eye at one end with a nail and drain the coconut water into a bowl. If the liquid tastes sweet and fragrant, the coconut is fresh. If it tastes oily and sour, the coconut is rancid and should be thrown away. Crack open the nut with the hammer and remove the oily, white flesh from the shell, peeling off the brown inner skin with a potato peeler. Canned coconut milk is the closest substitute for fresh coconut milk. It is produced by removing the shell, husk, and water and then pressing the fresh coconut flesh. Coconut cream is thicker than coconut milk because it contains less water, and creamed coconut, sold in blocks, is even more concentrated. These offer a slightly sweeter flavour to Indian dishes. Coconut powder is also available in Asian food stores and is a great cupboard standby for quick Indian curries and desserts.

Mango (aam)—Mangoes are considered the king of fruits in India. They come in hundreds of varieties and different sizes, with colours ranging from green to bright orange and red. The ripe fruit has a peachlike flesh, with a sweet and creamy taste and a perfumed aroma. Mangoes are used in chutneys, pickles, curries, drinks, and desserts and are eaten on their own.

Mung bean sprouts (moong)—In Maharashtra, Gujarat, and Andhra Pradesh, whole mung beans are sprouted and eaten as a salad (see page 164) or a first course. Sprouting the beans makes them much easier to digest (see page 18).

Okra (bhindi)—Of all the exotic vegetables, Indians love okra the most. Okra is also called gumbo or ladyfingers. The green skin is slightly fuzzy, and the flesh inside has rows of creamy white seeds. Okra must be washed and dried thoroughly before cooking. The pods should not be damp when you cut them, and you should not wash okra after you have cut it, or it will exude a sticky substance. Avoid okra with blemishes and choose firm, not mushy, pods with stems that snap cleanly.

HERBS, SPICES, AND FLAVORINGS

Ajowan seeds (ajowan)—Native to southern India, this seed is closely related to caraway and cumin, although it tastes strongly of thyme. It has a distinct, pungent aroma and a sharp taste so it is used in moderation. It is known for its carminative properties and is used, therefore, in rich, deep-fried preparations and bean recipes.

Asafoetida (hing)—Powerful and pungent, asafoetida is a dried, yellow-brown resin obtained from the roots of the fennel plant. The plants are native to Central Asia, from Iran to Afghanistan. Asafoetida is a spice generally used with vegetables rather than meat. So, although its natural habitat lies in the north, asafoetida is associated with South India, where vegetarianism is most common. Only a tiny amount is used for any dish—the resin is fried in hot oil so it can be easily dispersed throughout the other ingredients. The high temperature changes the taste, releasing an aroma that is reminiscent of raw onion and garlic. Asafoetida is used in legume dishes to ease the digestion of lentils and beans, as well as in curries, pickles, and chutneys.

Bay leaf (tej patta)—The type of bay leaf used in Indian cooking is the leaf of the cassia tree. These leaves are long, thin, and light green in color, with a mellow spicy aroma and a sweet taste. In Indian cooking, the bay leaf is used as a flavoring in meat and rice dishes, and it is an important component in the Moghul style of cuisine. One or two dried leaves are sufficient to scent a dish, and they can be removed easily before serving.

Black cardamom (badi elaichi)—Black cardamom is not true cardamom, but a related variety, the flavor and texture of which are not as delicate as those of the green cardamom. Dried black cardamom pods are actually dark brown in color, rough and ribbed on the surface. The oval pods are about 1 inch long. Peeling back the leathery skin releases a woody, smoky, camphoraceous aroma and reveals a mass of about 40 hard, sticky, tar-colored seeds encased in a soft, sweet-smelling pulp. An invaluable spice in any tandoori-style recipe of northern India, black cardamom is an important component in spice blends such as Garam Masala (see page 23). Unlike green cardamom, it is never used in sweet dishes, but is reserved solely for savoury cooking.

Cassia (dalchini)—Although closely related to cinnamon and often confused with it, cassia bark comes from Burma, while cinnamon's birthplace is Sri Lanka. Like cinnamon, cassia comes from the bark of an evergreen laurel tree. The bark is peeled from thin branches, then dried in the sun to form quills or cassia sticks. The aroma of cassia is highly perfumed, penetrating, sweet, and lingering. The flavor has an agreeable bitterness and is more robust than cinnamon. Cassia is used in Garam Masala (see page 23) and for flavoring rice dishes and curries, certain desserts, and Indian tea. Cinnamon can be used in place of cassia bark, but some supermarkets now stock cassia.

Chili (mirchi)—There are hundreds of varieties of chilies in the world, but Indian cooks tend to favor the long, slender, green variety. When buying fresh chilies, make sure the skins are smooth and shiny. The general rule of thumb is the smaller the chili, the hotter it is. The heat of the chili depends upon the amount of capsaicin, a volatile oil found in the seeds and the pith of the chili. The seeds of the chili can be removed and discarded if desired, but this will give a milder taste to the dish. For the recipes in this book, do not remove any of the seeds. Chili powder is a substitute for fresh green chilies and often a dish requires both. The heat of these blends varies, so it is worth testing in advance or using a small amount when you cook with them the first time. Large dried red chilies tend to be milder in heat than small ones. They are useful to have in your cupboard because they last longer than fresh ones. For the most flavor, chilies tend to be dry roasted or heated in oil before using.

Clove (laung)—Cloves are dark brown in color and have a sharp pungent taste and fragrant aroma. These dried unopened flower buds are bitter on their own, but the heat of the cooking tones down their flavors.

Coriander and Cilantro (dhania)—The plant *Coriandrum sativum* yields both the pungent-smelling spice known as coriander seed and the highly aromatic herb known as cilantro or coriander leaf. In Indian cooking, the seeds are an important component in the northern spice blend Garam Masala (see page 23) and are generally ground or crushed before use. Fresh cilantro leaves are used extensively in Indian cooking and as a garnish. They are best stored in the refrigerator in an airtight container and should always be rinsed well before use. The best way to clean cilantro is to place it in a bowl of cold water and swish it around with your hands to remove any grit or dirt particles.

Cumin seeds (jeera)—Greenish-yellow cumin seeds resemble caraway and are an integral part of Indian cooking. The slightly bitter, yet warming, flavor makes one think of curry. They have an earthy, warm, pungent aroma and taste pungent, spicy, and sweet.

Curry leaf (kari patta)—These small, shiny leaves, about 1-inch long, are used whole in Indian cooking, much like bay leaves. The leaves, which have a citrus scent, lend a dish a distinct curry aroma. Curry leaves are generally heated in oil to release their flavor. Once heated, they look shriveled and crispy. Fresh curry leaves can be stored in a sealed plastic bag in the refrigerator for up to 1 week.

Fennel seeds (saunf)—The greenish-yellow seeds of fennel resemble cumin but are slightly fatter and larger. They impart a strong anise flavor that is warm and menthol-like. It is one of the important spices in the East Indian spice mixture known as Panch Phoron (see page 24) and is also used to flavor drinks and sweets.

Fenugreek seeds (methi)—Rectangular in shape and brownish-yellow in color, fenugreek seeds are generally fried or toasted whole before use to reduce their bitterness. Ground fenugreek tastes strong, bitter, and intensely aromatic. It is used as a pickling spice and is one of the spices in the East Indian spice mixture Panch Phoron (see page 24).

Ginger (adrak)—Although a root, ginger is used like a spice. It adds a touch of heat to savory Indian dishes. The skin can be peeled with a knife or scraped off with a metal spoon before the root is grated or chopped. Look for pieces that are not wrinkled. Indians often add ginger at the end of cooking—the flavor is very strong when eaten almost raw.

Green cardamom (elaichi)—After saffron and vanilla, cardamom is the third most expensive spice in the world. Dried cardamom pods are pale green, oval, knobbly in shape, and about ½ inch long. When the peppery husk is crushed open, three seed segments, each containing three or four brown-black, oily, pungent seeds, are revealed. The taste of the seeds is warm and camphoraceous. Cardamom is used in both sweet and savory dishes and many spice blends, as well as Indian tea. Black cardamom pods are generally used whole in Indian cooking; however, the seeds of the green cardamom pods are often used on their own without the husks. To remove the seeds of green cardamom pods, place them on a flat surface and, using the back of a spoon, crush them until the casings split open. Green cardamom can also be used whole in spice mixtures, where the husks are ground along with the seeds.

Mango powder (amchur/amchoor)—Made from raw green mangoes that are cut, dried in the sun, and pounded into a powder, mango powder is used as a souring agent in Indian cooking, adding a tangy taste to dishes without adding moisture. It is often sprinkled over meat to tenderize it. Look for it in Asian food stores.

Mustard seeds (rai)—Mustard seeds come from three large shrubs, *Brassica juncea* (brown mustard), *B. nigra* (black mustard), and *B. hirta* (white mustard). All three produce bright yellow flowers that die off to leave small round seeds. The brown seeds, which are small, matte, and hard, are the ones predominantly used in Indian cooking. When heated they taste bitter, nutty, hot, and aromatic.

Nigella seeds (kalonji)—The *Nigella* plant is grown predominantly in India and although the seeds are also known as onion seeds, they have nothing to do with onions. The seeds have very little odor but release a scent similar to oregano when rubbed between your fingers. They have a nutty, bitter flavor and are one of the five spices in the East Indian blend known as Panch Phoron (see page 24). They are also added to bread doughs.

Pomegranate seeds (anardana)—These are the sun-dried fruit kernels of the plant *Punica granatum*. Pomegranate seeds are used extensively in the cuisines of the northern and northwestern regions, where they are often ground to impart a piquant flavor to snacks such as samosas and to curries.

Saffron (kesar)—Saffron is the dried stigma of *Crocus sativus*, a fall-flowering plant. More than 250,000 crocus flowers must be harvested to obtain 1 pound of saffron, and the stigmas need to be collected by hand, which is why saffron is the single most expensive spice. Almost all religious festival sweets and desserts are laced with saffron. It has a strong, penetrating, clinging aroma and a warm, rich, aromatic flavor. Steep the stigmas in water or milk for a few minutes before use to extract as much of the flavor as possible.

Tamarind (imli)—The tangy fruit of the tamarind tree grows in large, seeded, pulp-filled pods. Used to add tartness to Indian recipes, the pulp is available in an almost-black cake form resembling a pack of dates or in a liquid concentrate.

Turmeric (haldi)—Turmeric is the incredibly versatile spice that comes from the root of the *Curcuma longa*, a leafy plant belonging to the ginger family. It is mildly aromatic and tastes pungent, bitter, and earthy. Although often used as a substitute for saffron, the flavor is entirely different. In India, turmeric is used as a mild digestive and a remedy for liver ailments. It also possesses other medicinal qualities.

NUTS (DAANE)

Nuts are used in Indian cooking to thicken sauces, enrich desserts, garnish dishes, and create Indian sweets, such as the fudge known as barfi.

Almond (badaam)—The almond is the most important nut in Indian cooking. It is used to make velvety smooth sauces for curries, luscious desserts, and as a garnish for Moghul-style dishes.

Cashew nut (kaaju)—This kidney-shaped nut is found mainly in the cuisine of southern India. It is chopped, lightly fried, and added to both sweet and savory dishes, including curries, desserts, and snacks.

Pistachio (pista)—In addition to its use as a roasted, salty snack, the raw, unsalted pistachio is used in Indian cooking, especially in desserts, rice dishes, and Indian Milk Fudge (see page 179).

LEGUMES (DAL)

Legumes can be grouped into three broad categories: lentils, beans, and peas. There are hulled, split ones with the skin removed and unhulled varieties with the skin still intact. Lentils do not need soaking and are easier to cook than whole beans. Red and yellow lentils are actually split so they are even quicker to cook. This means that you cannot replace a split lentil with a whole bean in a recipe. It is acceptable to use canned legumes and beans for the recipes but make sure you drain and rinse them thoroughly before cooking. If using dried legumes, check through them for stones (this is especially important if you have bought them in bulk from a whole-food or Indian food store, but less so for those bought from a supermarket), then put them in a strainer and rinse under cold running water before cooking.

Bengal gram (chana dal/Bengal gram dal)—Closely related to the chickpea, *Bengal gram* is smaller, often split, and tastes sweeter, so it can be used to make Indian desserts. Bengal gram can be found in Asian food stores.

Black-eyed peas (chawli/lobhia/rongi)—Indians from the southwest use black-eyed peas in abundance, cooked in stews and braised in dishes with spices. In northern India, they are prepared in similar ways to kidney beans.

Dried beans—After lentils, dried beans are the second-most common legume consumed in India. They need soaking—and the longer you store them, the longer you need to cook them because they toughen with age. The green split mung bean (*moong dal*) is light and delicate when cooked, looking cream or yellow in color with flecks of green.

Lentils (dal)—The two most popular lentils in Indian cuisine, and the ones used in the recipes in this book, are yellow lentils (*tuvar* or *arhar dal*) and red lentils (*masoor dal*). Lentils are the easiest legumes to digest and the quickest to cook. Yellow lentils are sometimes sold with an oily coating that should be rinsed off before cooking.

CUPBOARD INGREDIENTS

Basmati rice (basmati chawal)—Basmati, meaning the queen of fragrance, is a long-grain rice grown in the foothills of the Himalayas. Once cooked, the grains stay firm and separate, are spongy to the touch, and exude an earthy and nutty aroma. There are several varieties and grades of basmati rice, which you might have to purchase and test before choosing the one that you personally like. Store rice and other grains in a cool, dry cupboard.

Chickpea or gram flour (besan)—This flour is pale yellow in color, silky in texture, and has a pleasant, nutty aroma. It is used in the preparation of both savory and sweet Indian dishes. Be careful not to confuse gram flour with graham flour, which is made from wheat. Like all flours, gram flour should be stored in a cool, dry place, away from direct sunlight, as exposure to heat can cause it to spoil and take on a stale, rancid taste.

Oils (tel)—The oils used in Indian cooking vary according to the regional style of cuisine, which is determined by a region's climate and geography. Most dishes are cooked in vegetable oil. In northern India, peanut oil is traditionally used for frying; in the east, it is mustard oil; and in the south, coconut oil is favored. The recipes in this book use mostly vegetable oil and, occasionally, peanut oil, which you will find in supermarkets and Asian food stores.

Poppadums (papad)—Poppadums are thin wafers made from ground lentils, oil, and spices and are served as a cocktail accompaniment or simply as a snack. To deep-fry them, immerse them one at a time into vegetable oil heated to 350–400°F 4 to 5 seconds until they crinkle and expand, turning a pale gold color. Remove the poppadums immediately from the oil, shake off the excess, and drain on kitchen paper. Alternatively, you can brush both sides of the poppadum with a little oil and place it under a medium-hot broiler, turning it once when brown spots appear on one side. Once cooked, poppadums can be served right away, or stored in an airtight container at room temperature 5 to 6 days.

Rice flour (Chawal ka atta)—Rice flour is a fine white powder made from grinding white long-grain rice. Free from gluten, it is often used in Indian cooking as an alternative to wheat flour to make Indian-style flatbreads such as South Indian *appams* or soft breads. Rice flour also acts as a binding and thickening agent. You can make your own rice flour by pulverizing uncooked Basmati rice grains in an electric grinder, but it is also available in specialty food stores and in most supermarkets.

TECHNIQUES

CHOPPING MANGOES

Use a sharp knife to slice the flesh away from the central seed, to yield two thick pieces. Make crisscross cuts in the flesh without cutting through the peel, then bend the peel back and carefully cut the flesh away from it. Don't forget to cut away any flesh from around the seed.

DRY ROASTING SPICES (BHUNA)

Dry-roast, or toast, spices by warming them in a hot, dry pan over medium-low heat until they release their aroma. Watch carefully so they do not burn and tip them out of the pan as soon as you can smell the aroma. This method enhances the flavors of the spices. After they cool, they are usually ground to a powder. This procedure is also used in making various spice mixtures such as Garam Masala (see page 23). The spices are then ready for use in Indian dishes.

FRYING SPICES (TAKDA/BAGHAR)

Heat some oil or melt some ghee or butter in a hot pan and add the spices, which are often whole but sometimes ground. Fry them until they splutter and sizzle. They shouldn't burn. This process, which intensifies the flavors of a dish, is either carried out as the first step in cooking, before adding the onions, for example, or as the last stage when this spice-perfumed oil is then added to a dish as a final touch or a garnish. The garnishing technique is often used for lentil dishes, chutneys, salads, and vegetable recipes.

PEELING TOMATOES

With a small, sharp knife, cut a cross in the skin at the bottom of the tomato. Place it in a heatproof bowl, pour boiling water over to cover, and set aside 30 seconds. Use a slotted spoon to remove the tomato, then use the knife to peel.

REMOVING SHRIMP VEINS

Cut along the back of the shrimp using a small, sharp knife, without cutting all the way through. Lift out the dark digestive tract, using the tip of the knife, then remove any remnants of the vein under cold running water.

SPROUTING MUNG BEANS

Rinse the mung beans, then put them in a bowl, cover with warm water, and set aside at least 8 hours or overnight. Drain and rinse the beans, put them in a piece of clean, damp cheesecloth and tie it to enclose them. Leave in a warm place for another 8 hours, or until the outer casings of the beans begin to crack and tiny white sprouts appear. Sprinkle with a little warm water once or twice while the beans are sprouting in the cloth to prevent them from drying out. Rinse the sprouted beans and use immediately, or wrap in a clean, damp cloth and refrigerate until required. However, they need to be cooked within 48 hours.

CHUTNEYS AND SPICE MIXTURES

MANGO CHUTNEY
AAM KI CHUTNEY

SERVES 4
PREPARATION TIME: 10 MINUTES
COOKING TIME: 15 MINUTES

Chutneys in India tend to be sharp and sour and are served with a main meal or as a side relish for savory snacks. Although there are countless commercial mango chutneys available, it is rare to find one with noticeable thick chunks of fruit throughout.

3 tablespoons **vegetable oil**

1 large ripe **mango**, peeled and roughly chopped (*see page 18*)

1-inch piece **gingerroot**, peeled and grated

2 tablespoons **sugar**

1 tablespoon **malt vinegar**

1½ teaspoons **chili powder**

1½ teaspoons **salt**

1 **HEAT** the oil in a heavy-bottomed saucepan over low heat.

2 **ADD** the mango, ginger, sugar, vinegar, chili powder, and salt and cook, stirring occasionally, 15 minutes, or until the mango is soft.

3 **REMOVE** the pan from the heat and let the chutney cool completely.

4 **TRANSFER** the cool chutney to an airtight container and refrigerate up to 2 weeks.

MINT AND YOGURT CHUTNEY
PUDINA RAITA

SERVES 4
PREPARATION TIME: 10 MINUTES

2 **green chilies**, roughly chopped

a generous handful **mint leaves**

1 bunch **cilantro leaves**, roughly chopped

1 **onion**, roughly chopped

¼ cup **plain yogurt**

1 tablespoon **lemon juice**

½ teaspoon **salt**

1 **PUT** all of the ingredients in a blender and blend until the mixture forms a thick, coarse paste.

2 **TRANSFER** the chutney to an airtight container and refrigerate up to 4 days.

VARIATION

CILANTRO CHUTNEY—Put 2 bunches roughly chopped cilantro leaves, 2 chopped green chilies, 1 teaspoon lemon juice, 1 teaspoon sugar, and ½ teaspoon salt in a blender and blend until a fine paste forms. Add 2 tablespoons water if the mixture seems too dry. Transfer to an airtight container and refrigerate up to 4 days.

COCONUT AND TOMATO CHUTNEY

MYSORE CHUTNEY

SERVES 4
PREPARATION TIME: 10 MINUTES
COOKING TIME: 5 MINUTES

Fresh coconut marks this flavorsome chutney with a subtle sweetness that is nicely balanced by the heat of the dried chilies. If fresh coconut is not available, unsweetened shredded coconut makes a suitable substitute.

2 tablespoons **tamarind pulp**

2 tablespoons **peanut oil**

6 **dried red chilies**, stems removed

2 **tomatoes**, roughly chopped

½ **coconut** (about 7 ounces), peeled and broken into pieces

½ teaspoon **salt**

6 **curry leaves**

½ teaspoon **brown mustard seeds**

½ teaspoon **cumin seeds**

a pinch **asafoetida**

1 PUT the tamarind pulp in a heatproof bowl, pour over enough boiling water to cover, and let stand 10 minutes. Use a wooden spoon to press the pulp and release the fibers and seeds, then strain through a nylon strainer into a bowl, using the back of the spoon to extract as much juice as possible. Discard the tamarind pulp and set aside the juice.

2 HEAT 1 tablespoon of the oil in a skillet over medium heat. Add the chilies and fry, stirring constantly, 30 seconds, or until they sizzle. Watch the chilies carefully so they do not burn.

3 TRANSFER the chilies to a blender with the tomatoes, coconut, salt, tamarind juice, and 2 tablespoons water and blend until a fairly smooth paste forms. Pour the chutney into a bowl and set aside. Wipe out the skillet the chilies were fried in.

4 HEAT the remaining 1 tablespoon oil in the skillet over medium heat. Add the curry leaves, mustard seeds, cumin seeds, and asafoetida and fry, stirring constantly, 30 seconds, or until the seeds begin to splutter. Watch carefully so they do not burn.

5 SPOON this mixture over the coconut and tomato chutney and stir well. The chutney is now ready to serve or it can be left to cool, transferred to an airtight container, and refrigerated 3 to 4 days. Remove it from the refrigerator about 10 minutes before serving so the flavor of the coconut isn't masked by the cold.

TOMATO CHUTNEY

TAMATAR CHUTNEY

SERVES 4
PREPARATION TIME: **10** MINUTES, PLUS COOLING TIME
COOKING TIME: **12** MINUTES

*Tomato and tamarind combine to create a tangy, aromatic chutney.
This recipe works just as well with canned tomatoes, if fresh ones
are not in season.*

2 tablespoons **tamarind pulp**

1 pound **tomatoes**, peeled (*see page 18*) and chopped

2 **garlic** cloves, chopped

1 teaspoon **sugar**

1 teaspoon **chili powder**

1 teaspoon **salt**

¼ teaspoon **turmeric**

1 tablespoon **peanut oil**

6 **curry leaves**

¼ teaspoon **brown mustard seeds**

a pinch **asafoetida**

1 PUT the tamarind pulp in a heatproof bowl, pour
over enough boiling water to cover, and let stand
10 minutes. Use a wooden spoon to press the pulp
and release the fibers and seeds, then strain through
a nylon strainer into a bowl, using the back of the
spoon to extract as much juice as possible. Discard the
tamarind pulp and set aside the juice.

2 PUT the tomatoes in a large saucepan over medium
heat. Add the garlic, sugar, chili powder, salt, turmeric,
and tamarind juice and bring to a boil, stirring. Reduce the
heat to low and simmer 10 minutes, stirring occasionally,
to blend the flavors and thicken. Remove the pan from
the heat and set aside until the chutney cools completely.

3 TRANSFER the chutney to a blender and blend until
a smooth paste forms. Spoon the chutney into a glass jar
with a tight-fitting, nonmetallic lid but do not close.

4 HEAT the oil in a skillet over medium heat. Add the
curry leaves, mustard seeds, and asafoetida and fry,
stirring constantly, 30 seconds, or until the seeds splutter.
Watch carefully so they do not burn.

5 STIR the spice mixture into the chutney. The chutney
is now ready to use, or it can be left to cool in the glass jar,
then sealed and refrigerated up to 2 weeks.

CUCUMBER RELISH

KHEERA RAITA

SERVES 4
PREPARATION TIME: 5 MINUTES, PLUS CHILLING

A raita is a yogurt-based condiment usually containing vegetables. Raitas are designed to be cooling, to counteract the effects of any spicy hot dishes. So, if you find a curry too fiery, balance the heat with a milk-based preparation such as this one.

½ **cucumber**, coarsely grated

1¼ cups **plain yogurt**, whisked

¼ teaspoon **salt**

¼ teaspoon **ground cumin**

a pinch freshly ground **black pepper**

a pinch **chili powder**

1 SQUEEZE any excess water from the grated cucumber, using your hands.

2 PLACE the cucumber in a bowl, then stir in the yogurt.

3 STIR in the salt, cumin, black pepper, and chili powder. Cover the bowl with plastic wrap and refrigerate until required. Serve chilled.

VARIATION

ONION AND YOGURT RELISH—Put 1¼ cups plain yogurt in a large bowl and whisk until smooth. Stir in 1 chopped onion, 1 finely chopped green chili, and ¼ teaspoon salt. Heat 1 tablespoon vegetable oil in a skillet over medium heat. Add 6 curry leaves and ¼ teaspoon brown mustard seeds and fry, stirring constantly, until the spices splutter. Watch carefully so they do not burn. Immediately tip the mixture into the yogurt and stir well. Cover the bowl with plastic wrap and refrigerate until required. Serve chilled.

GARLIC, YOGURT, AND PEANUT RELISH—Put 1¼ cups plain yogurt in a large bowl and whisk until smooth. Stir in 2 peeled and crushed garlic cloves, 1 finely chopped green chili, ¼ teaspoon salt, and a handful finely chopped cilantro leaves. Heat 1 tablespoon vegetable oil in a skillet over medium heat and add 10 to 15 skinned and unsalted crushed peanuts. Fry 1 minute, or until the peanuts turn golden brown. Turn off the heat and let cool. Stir the peanuts into the yogurt relish, cover the bowl with plastic wrap, and refrigerate until required. Serve chilled.

LEMON PICKLE
NIMBU KA ACHAAR

SERVES 4
PREPARATION TIME: 10 MINUTES, PLUS 30 MINUTES SOAKING TIME
AND 1 WEEK MATURING TIME

Most Indian pickles are prepared with various spices and oil, rather than vinegar. The oil in this recipe comes from the skin of the lemons.

12 **lemons**
½ cup **salt**
1½ cups **sugar**
1 tablespoon **ajowan seeds**
6 **dried red chilies**

1 WASH the lemons, then let them soak in cold water to cover 30 minutes. Dry the lemons, then top and tail them and cut each into 8 pieces.
2 PLACE the lemons and the remaining ingredients in a nonmetallic bowl and mix together.
3 TRANSFER the pickle mixture to a large glass jar with a nonmetallic lid, seal, and let rest in a warm place 1 week before using.
4 SHAKE the jar gently at least once a day to ensure the liquid released from the lemons covers the lemons. When the lemons begin to turn dark, the pickle is ready to eat. Refrigerate after opening. The pickle will keep up to 3 months in the refrigerator.

GARAM MASALA
GARAM MASALA

MAKES ABOUT 5 TABLESPOONS
PREPARATION TIME: 5 MINUTES
COOKING TIME: 2 MINUTES

Garam masala *quite literally means a mixture of hot spices and is a blend of dry-roasted whole spices from northern India that are ground to a powder. Garam masala is usually added at the end of cooking to finish off a dish with a delicate aroma of roasted spices, but it can also be added with other spices during cooking. Once you've made this, you'll find there is no comparison between a fresh blend you make at home and the store-bought varieties that have been sitting on a shelf for months.*

4 pieces **cinnamon stick** or **cassia bark**, each 2-inches long
12 **bay leaves**
5 **black cardamom pods**
20 **green cardamom pods**
2 tablespoons **coriander seeds**
2 tablespoons **cumin seeds**
1 teaspoon **cloves**
1 teaspoon **black peppercorns**

1 HEAT a dry skillet over medium-low heat until you can feel the heat rising. Add the cinnamon stick or cassia bark, bay leaves, and black cardamom and roast for 30 seconds, shaking the pan.
2 ADD the remaining spices and continue roasting, shaking the pan, for about 1 minute longer, or until you can smell

the aroma of the spices. Watch carefully so they
do not burn.

3 REMOVE the pan from the heat and immediately
tip the spices onto a plate and let cool completely.

4 TRANSFER the spices to a spice mill and blend until
finely ground. Store the mixture in an airtight container,
away from direct sunlight, up to 6 months.

VARIATIONS

PANCH PHORON—Heat a dry skillet over medium-low
heat. Add 4 dried red chilies, ½ teaspoon *each* brown mustard
seeds, fenugreek seeds, nigella seeds, and fennel seeds and
roast, shaking the pan constantly, about 3 minutes, or until
you can smell the aroma. Watch carefully so the seeds do
not burn. Let cool completely, then grind and store as above.

DHANSAK MASALA—Heat a dry skillet over medium-
low heat. Add a 2-inch piece cinnamon stick or cassia bark,
20 green cardamom pods, 2 teaspoons *each* cumin and
coriander seeds, 1 teaspoon *each* black peppercorns,
brown mustard seeds, and fenugreek seeds, 4 bay leaves,
and ½ teaspoon *each* cloves and turmeric. Roast, shaking
the pan constantly, about 3 minutes, or until you can smell
the aroma of the spices. Watch carefully so they do not burn.
Let cool completely, then grind and store as above.

MANJU'S QUICK CURRY PASTE
MANJU KI JHATPAT MASALA

MAKES 6½ TABLESPOONS
PREPARATION TIME: 5 MINUTES

*This blend of spices and other ingredients is used to create a flavorful
curry sauce. This paste provides a base to a medium-hot, tangy curry.*

2 tablespoons **vegetable oil**

2 teaspoons **tomato paste**

2 teaspoons **ground cumin**

2 teaspoons **ground coriander**

1 teaspoon **turmeric**

½ teaspoon **Garam Masala** (*see page 23*)

¼ teaspoon **chili powder**

¼ teaspoon **salt**

1 MIX all the ingredients in a small bowl to form a thick,
reddish-brown paste.

2 USE at once, or transfer to an airtight container and
refrigerate up to 9 days.

MADRAS CURRY PASTE
GEELA MASALA

MAKES 7 TO 8 TABLESPOONS
PREPARATION TIME: 10 MINUTES, PLUS COOLING TIME
COOKING TIME: 7 MINUTES

The pungent coriander and cumin, spicy black pepper, and nutty brown mustard featured in this curry paste create an authentic taste of southern India.

1 tablespoon **black peppercorns**

4 tablespoons **coriander seeds**

2 tablespoons **cumin seeds**

1 teaspoon **brown mustard seeds**

½ cup **vegetable oil**

6 **garlic** cloves, crushed

2-inch piece **gingerroot**, peeled and chopped

1 tablespoon **chili powder**

1 tablespoon **turmeric**

1 **HEAT** a dry skillet over medium-low heat. Add the peppercorns and the coriander, cumin, and mustard seeds and roast, shaking the pan occasionally, until you can smell the aroma. Watch the spices carefully so they do not burn. Remove the pan from the heat and immediately tip the spices onto a plate and let cool completely.

2 **TRANSFER** the spices to a spice mill and blend until finely ground, then set aside.

3 **POUR** the oil into a saucepan over medium heat. Add the garlic, ginger, chili powder, and turmeric and stir well. Add the freshly ground spices and fry, stirring constantly, 30 seconds to 1 minute until the oil separates.

4 **REMOVE** the pan from the heat and let the paste cool completely. Transfer the paste to an airtight container and store, away from direct sunlight, up to 6 months.

VARIATION

GREEN MASALA PASTE—Heat a dry skillet over medium-low heat, add a 2-inch piece cinnamon stick or cassia bark, 9 black peppercorns, 4 cloves, and 1 teaspoon cumin seeds and roast until you can smell the aroma. Watch the spices carefully so they do not burn. Immediately tip the spices onto a plate and let cool completely, then put them in a spice mill and blend until finely ground, then transfer to a blender. Add a 2-inch piece peeled and chopped gingerroot, 5 chopped garlic cloves, 2 chopped green chilies, 1 chopped onion, a handful cilantro leaves, 9 mint leaves, 2 tablespoons vegetable oil, 1 tablespoon lemon juice, and ¼ teaspoon salt and blend until a coarse, light green paste forms. Store as above.

BREADS

NAANS
NAANS

MAKES 4   PREPARATION TIME: 15 MINUTES, PLUS AT LEAST
30 MINUTES RISING TIME   COOKING TIME: 10 TO 15 MINUTES

Naan, *the Persian word for bread, refers in Indian cooking to this oval flatbread made with white wheat flour and usually leavened with yeast. Milk or yogurt is added for greater volume. Naans are traditionally made in a tandoor—a large, charcoal-heated, bowl-shaped oven. The breads are placed on the inside walls of the oven and baked in minutes. Although tandoor-baked naans are more rustic looking and larger than those made in a domestic oven, yours will taste the same. Naans can be cooked the day before, stored in an airtight container, and reheated in an oven at 350°F 5 minutes. To prevent them from drying out, sprinkle them with a few drops of water and wrap them in foil before reheating.*

1 teaspoon **active dry yeast**

1 teaspoon **sugar**

1½ cups **all-purpose flour**, plus extra for dusting

½ teaspoon **baking powder**

¼ teaspoon **salt**

1 tablespoon **vegetable oil**, plus extra for greasing
    the baking sheet

2 tablespoons **plain yogurt**

2 tablespoons **milk**

1 PUT the yeast in a small bowl and stir in 1 tablespoon warm water. Stir in the sugar and set aside in a warm place, uncovered, 5 minutes, or until bubbles appear and the mixture looks a little frothy.

2 COMBINE the flour, baking powder, and salt in a large bowl. Make a well in the middle. Pour the oil, yogurt, and milk into the well, then add the yeast mixture. Mix until a soft dough forms. If the dough is dry and doesn't come together, sprinkle 1 to 2 tablespoons water over.

3 KNEAD the dough by clenching your hand into a fist, then wet your knuckles and press them repeatedly into the dough, pressing against the side of the bowl, until a soft, smooth dough forms. This should take about 10 minutes.

4 COVER the bowl with a clean, damp dish towel or plastic wrap and set aside in a warm place to rise until the dough increases in volume and is no longer sticky. This will take at least 30 minutes, but, ideally, let it rise 3 to 4 hours.

5 PREHEAT the oven to 400°F and lightly grease a baking sheet large enough to hold 4 naans.

6 PUNCH down the dough, then divide it into 4 balls of equal size. Lightly flour the countertop and roll each ball into a long, oval shape about ¼-inch thick. Do not roll them too thin, or they will be too crispy.

7 PUT the naans on the baking sheet, place them in the middle of the oven, and bake 10 to 12 minutes until they puff up slightly and are golden and flaky. Serve hot.

EXOTIC LEAVENED NAANS

PESHWARI NAANS

MAKES **4**   PREPARATION TIME: **15** MINUTES, PLUS AT LEAST
30 MINUTES RISING TIME   COOKING TIME: **10–15** MINUTES

The Peshwari naan is a popular variation on the traditional plain naan (see left). These breads, thought to have come from Peshawar, in Pakistan, are filled with a mixture of nuts and dried fruits. This recipe includes shredded coconut, a popular ingredient in the Peshwari naans in Western restaurants, although not commonly used in Pakistan. Most traditional recipes use yeast, but self-rising flour is used here for more convenience.

vegetable oil for greasing the baking sheet

1⅓ cups **self-rising flour**, plus extra for dusting

¼ cup **light cream**

2 tablespoons **plain yogurt**

1 tablespoon **ground almonds**

1 tablespoon **shredded coconut**

1 tablespoon **sugar**

1 tablespoon **golden raisins**

1 PREHEAT the oven to 400°F and lightly grease a baking sheet large enough to hold 4 naans.

2 PLACE the flour in a large mixing bowl and make a well in the middle. Pour the cream, yogurt, and 3 tablespoons water into the well and mix until a soft dough forms. If the dough is dry and doesn't come together, sprinkle with 1 to 2 tablespoons water.

3 KNEAD the dough by clenching your hand into a fist, then wet your knuckles and press them repeatedly into the dough, pressing against the side of the bowl, until a soft, pliable dough forms. This should take about 10 minutes.

4 COVER the bowl with a clean, damp dish towel or plastic wrap and set aside in a warm place to rise until the dough increases in volume and is no longer sticky. This will take at least 30 minutes.

5 DIVIDE the dough into 4 balls of equal size. Lightly dust the countertop with flour and roll each ball into a long, oval shape about ¼-inch thick. Do not roll them too thin, or they will be too crispy.

6 COMBINE the ground almonds, shredded coconut, sugar, and golden raisins in a bowl. Sprinkle this mixture along the middle of each piece of dough, then fold the dough over to enclose the filling. Press the edges together to seal. Reroll each piece into a long, oval shape.

7 PUT the naans on the greased baking sheet, place them on the middle shelf of the oven, and bake 10 to 12 minutes until they puff up slightly and are golden and flaky. Serve hot.

FENUGREEK FLATBREADS

GUJARATI THEPLAS

MAKES 6   PREPARATION TIME: 8 MINUTES, PLUS 15 TO 30 MINUTES
RESTING TIME   COOKING TIME: 12 MINUTES

*These unleavened flatbreads from Gujarat, in western India, are similar
to chapatis. The dough is prepared with wholewheat flour and chickpea
or gram flour, which adds nuttiness and extra flavor.*

1 cup **wholewheat flour**, plus extra for dusting

¼ cup **chickpea** or **gram flour**

a pinch **asafoetida**

a handful **fenugreek leaves**, chopped, or 2 tablespoons
   dried fenugreek leaves

½ teaspoon **turmeric**

½ teaspoon **cumin seeds**

¼ teaspoon **chili powder**

¼ teaspoon **ground coriander**

¼ teaspoon **salt**

3 tablespoons **vegetable oil**

1 PUT the wholewheat and chickpea or gram flours,
   asafoetida, fenugreek leaves, turmeric, cumin seeds, chili
   powder, coriander, and salt in a large bowl and mix well.

2 MAKE a well in the middle. Add 1 tablespoon of the
   oil to the well, then gradually add ½ cup warm water

and stir until the mixture forms a soft dough. If the dough
is dry and doesn't come together, sprinkle with 1 to 2
tablespoons water.

3 KNEAD the dough by clenching your hand into a fist,
then wet your knuckles and press them repeatedly into the
dough, pressing against the side of the bowl, until a soft,
smooth dough forms. This should take 5 to 6 minutes.

4 COVER the bowl with a clean, damp dish towel or plastic
wrap and set aside in a warm place to rest 15 to 30 minutes.

5 DIVIDE the dough into 6 balls of equal size. Dust each ball
with flour and roll it into a 6-inch circle. Dusting each
flatbread with a little flour as you roll it out prevents it from
sticking and allows the rolling pin to move freely.

6 HEAT a shallow skillet over medium heat until a splash
of water sizzles on the surface. Brush the surface with
1 teaspoon of the oil. Place a flatbread in the pan and cook
30 seconds to 1 minute, pressing down firmly all over
the surface with the back of a tablespoon.

7 FLIP the flatbread over, using tongs, and continue cooking
1 minute, carefully pressing down firmly so the dough
cooks all the way through and brown spots appear.

8 REMOVE the flatbread from the pan and wrap it in
a clean dish towel. Continue cooking the remaining flatbreads in the same way, brushing the surface of the pan
with 1 teaspoon oil before placing each flatbread in the
pan. Serve warm.

CHAPATIS
CHAPATIS

MAKES 6
PREPARATION TIME: 10 MINUTES
COOKING TIME: 6 TO 8 MINUTES

Chapatis, made fresh every day, are a type of unleavened bread from northern India. The wholewheat dough is rolled into flat circles and then cooked on a hot, flat griddle called a tava. In an Indian meal, chapatis are used as a scoop to pick up vegetable and lentil dishes.

1¾ cups **wholewheat flour**, plus extra for dusting
1 teaspoon **vegetable oil**
butter or **ghee**, melted, to serve (optional)

1 SIFT the flour into a large bowl, adding in the bran left in the sifter. Make a well in the middle. Add the oil to the well, then gradually add ⅔ cup warm water. Stir until the mixture forms a soft dough. If the dough is dry and does not come together, add 1 to 2 tablespoons water.

2 KNEAD the dough by clenching your hand into a fist, then wet your knuckles and press them repeatedly into the dough, pressing against the side of the bowl, until a soft, smooth dough forms. This should take about 10 minutes.

3 DIVIDE the dough into 6 balls of equal size. Dust each chapati with a little flour to prevent it from sticking, and so the rolling pin can move freely, then roll them out on a lightly floured surface into 6-inch circles.

4 HEAT a shallow skillet over medium heat until a splash of water sizzles on the surface.

5 PLACE a chapati in the pan and cook 20 seconds, or until the top surface starts to brown slightly.

6 TURN the chapati over, using tongs, and continue cooking about 30 seconds until the surface is bubbly.

7 FLIP the chapati over again and, using the back of a tablespoon, press firmly around the edge so it puffs up.

8 REMOVE the chapati from the pan and put it on a clean dish towel. Brush with the melted butter or ghee, if using, then wrap it in the towel to keep warm while you cook the remaining chapatis one at a time. Serve warm.

VARIATION
ONION AND CHILI CHAPATIS—Prepare the Chapatis recipe through step 3, then add 1 small, finely chopped onion, 2 finely chopped green chilies, and 1 teaspoon ajowan seeds to the dough. Knead 2 minutes longer, or until the ingredients are well combined. Follow the Chapatis recipe from step 4 to complete.

POORIS
POORIS

MAKES **8**
PREPARATION TIME: **10** MINUTES
COOKING TIME: **8** MINUTES

These deep-fried unleavened breads are served in Indian fast-food restaurants and are made at home during auspicious celebrations. They are served with either sweet or savory dishes, such as the tangy Shrimp Pooris (see page 60). In eastern India, pooris are also prepared at breakfast.

1½ cups **all-purpose flour**

1 tablespoon **butter**, softened

vegetable oil for deep-frying, plus extra

   for greasing the countertop

1 SIFT the flour into a large bowl, then add the butter and ¼ cup warm water. Mix until a soft dough forms.

2 KNEAD the dough by clenching your hand into a fist, then wet your knuckles and press them repeatedly into the dough, pressing against the side of the bowl, until a soft, pliable dough forms. This should take about 10 minutes.

3 DIVIDE the dough into 8 equal pieces and cover with a clean, damp dish towel. Lightly grease the countertop. Heat the oil in a deep saucepan or deep-fat fryer until it reaches 375°F, or until a small piece of the dough puffs up and rises to the surface instantly.

4 ROLL out one piece of dough into a circle 5 to 6 inches across and about ⅛-inch thick.

5 PLACE the rolled out dough in the hot oil. Fry 30 seconds, or until it puffs up. Use a slotted spoon to turn the poori over, then continue frying until it turns light brown.

6 REMOVE the poori from the oil with the slotted spoon, then drain well on a paper towel, taking care not to squash out too much air. Roll out another dough circle and repeat the process until you have rolled out and fried all the poori dough. These pooris can be made in advance and reheated in an oven at 350°F 5 minutes before serving. Serve hot.

VARIATION

SAMOSA PASTRY DOUGH—The dough used to make meat- and vegetable-filled samosas is the same as poori dough, except you substitute 2 teaspoons vegetable oil for the butter. Follow the recipe above through step 3, then roll out, shape, and fill the dough as explained in the Vegetable Samosa recipe on page 36.

RICE

PLAIN BASMATI RICE
BASMATI CHAWAL

SERVES **4**
PREPARATION TIME: **10** MINUTES, PLUS **5** MINUTES STANDING TIME
COOKING TIME: **10** TO **12** MINUTES

The mild taste of plain basmati rice harmonizes well with the aromatic, spicy, and often rich flavors of Indian cuisine. The absorption method of cooking rice, used here, is more streamlined than boiling the rice in a copious amount of water and then draining it. With the absorption method, all the water should be absorbed by the time the rice is tender. After cooking, the grains stay firm and separate and are not sticky.

Rice bought from a specialist Asian store can be soaked 20 to 30 minutes before cooking. This allows the grains to absorb water so that the heat penetrates more easily and the rice cooks evenly. Rice bought from a supermarket should be prepared according to the instructions on the package. Rice can be cooked up to 48 hours in advance, but should only be reheated once. It can be reheated over very low heat in the same pan, covered, with ¼ cup water. Or, cover it with foil and place it in a preheated oven at 350°F 10 minutes.

2 cups **basmati rice**

½ teaspoon **vegetable oil**

a pinch **salt**

1 BRING 3⅓ cups water to a boil. Put the rice in a strainer and rinse it under cold running water until the water runs clear. This will remove any excess starch.

2 PUT the rice in a saucepan, cover with a tight-fitting lid, and place over high heat.

3 STIR the oil, salt, and boiling water into the rice and then return to a boil.

4 COVER the pan, reduce the heat to low, and simmer 10 to 12 minutes. Do not uncover the pan before the rice has cooked at least 10 minutes. The rice will be tender when all the water is absorbed, holes appear on the surface, and some of the grains appear to be pointing up. Test a few grains to make sure the rice is tender. If, at the end of cooking, it is cooked but some of the water remains, drain the rice in a strainer. If the rice is not cooked and all the water has been absorbed, add ¼ cup boiling water, re-cover the pan with the lid, and cook 5 minutes longer.

5 FLUFF the rice with a fork, then cover the pan again and let stand 5 minutes. Serve piping hot.

VARIATION
SWEET RICE

Follow the Plain Basmati Rice recipe through step 4. Put 2 tablespoons milk and 10 saffron strands in a small bowl and let infuse 3 to 4 minutes. Melt 5 tablespoons butter or ghee over medium-high heat in a large saucepan. Add 4 cloves, 4 whole green cardamom pods, 10 coarsely chopped almonds, 10 coarsely chopped pistachio nuts, and, if you like, 1 tablespoon golden raisins. Stir 1 minute, then add the cooked rice and continue to stir 2 minutes. Stir in ¼ cup sugar and the saffron milk and stir another minute. Serve hot or cold as a dessert.

SPICED RICE

PULAO

SERVES 4
PREPARATION TIME: 7 MINUTES
COOKING TIME: 15 MINUTES

Pulaos are dishes in which every grain of the cooked rice remains separate. This recipe and the variations below are associated with the cooking of the Moghuls—Persian Muslim princes who ruled India for almost 200 years from the 16th century.

2 tablespoons **milk**

20 **saffron strands**

2 cups **basmati rice**

2 tablespoons **butter** or **ghee**

2-inch piece **cinnamon stick** or **cassia bark**

6 **black peppercorns**

4 **cloves**

4 **green cardamom pods**

2 **black cardamom pods**

2 **bay leaves**

¼ teaspoon **cumin seeds**

¼ teaspoon **salt**

1 PUT the milk and saffron strands in a small bowl and let infuse 3 to 4 minutes. Bring 2 cups water to a boil.

2 PUT the rice in a strainer and rinse under cold water until the water runs clear. This will remove any excess starch.

3 MELT the butter or ghee in a saucepan with a tight-fitting lid over low heat. Add the cinnamon stick or cassia bark, peppercorns, cloves, green and black cardamom pods, bay leaves, cumin seeds, and salt and stir 30 seconds, or until you can smell the aroma of the spices. Watch carefully so the spices do not burn.

4 ADD the rice to the pan and fry, stirring, 30 seconds.

5 POUR the boiling water into the pan, stir once, and then return to a boil. Cover the pan, reduce the heat to low, and simmer 3 minutes.

6 STIR the saffron-flavored milk into the rice.

7 PLACE the lid on the pan and simmer 7 to 9 minutes. Do not uncover the pan before the rice has cooked at least 7 minutes. The rice will be tender when all the liquid is absorbed, holes appear on the surface, and some of the grains appear to be pointing up. Test a few grains to make sure the rice is tender.

8 FLUFF the rice with a fork, then re-cover the pan, and let stand 5 minutes. Serve piping hot.

VARIATIONS

PULAO RICE WITH PEAS—Omit the saffron-flavored milk. Replace the butter or ghee with 2 tablespoons vegetable oil and heat over medium heat. Add a 2-inch piece cinnamon stick and 4 green cardamom pods and fry, stirring, 30 seconds, or until you can smell the aroma. Watch so the spices do not burn. Stir in 1 cup shelled peas, 1 chopped green chili, and ¼ teaspoon salt, then follow the Spiced Rice recipe from step 4, using 2 cups basmati rice. Once you reduce the heat and cover the pan, do not uncover for at least 10 minutes.

SAFFRON RICE—Put 2 tablespoons milk and 20 saffron strands in a small bowl and let infuse 3 to 4 minutes. Melt the butter or ghee over medium-high heat. Add 4 cloves, 4 green cardamom pods, and ¼ teaspoon *each* cumin seeds and salt. Fry, stirring constantly, 30 seconds, or until you can smell the aroma. Watch so the spices do not burn. Add 1 sliced onion and continue frying 3 minutes, or until the onion is soft, then follow the Spiced Rice recipe from step 4, using 2 cups basmati rice and adding the saffron-flavored milk to the pan after the rice.

TAMARIND RICE—Put the tamarind pulp in a heatproof bowl, pour enough boiling water to cover over, and let stand 10 minutes. Use a wooden spoon to press the pulp and release the fibers and seeds, then strain through a nylon strainer into a bowl, using the back of the spoon to extract as much juice as possible. Discard the tamarind pulp and set aside the juice. Omit the saffron-flavored milk from the Spiced Rice recipe. Replace the butter or ghee with 2 tablespoons peanut oil and heat over medium heat. Add ½ teaspoon brown mustard seeds, 2 dried red chilies, 1 teaspoon hulled split black lentils, a pinch of asafoetida, 6 curry leaves, and

¼ teaspoon salt. Fry, stirring constantly, 30 seconds, or until you can smell the aroma. Watch so the spices do not burn. Stir in the tamarind juice, then follow the Spiced Rice recipe from step 4, using 2 cups basmati rice. Once you reduce the heat and cover the pan, do not uncover for at least 10 minutes.

TURMERIC RICE—Omit the saffron-flavored milk. Replace the butter or ghee with 2 tablespoons vegetable oil and heat over medium heat. Add 1 teaspoon turmeric, ½ teaspoon *each* brown mustard seeds and cumin seeds, and ¼ teaspoon salt. Fry, stirring constantly, 30 seconds, or until you can smell the aroma. Watch so the spices do not burn. Follow the Spiced Rice recipe from step 4, using 2 cups basmati rice. Once you reduce the heat and cover the pan, do not uncover for at least 10 minutes.

PART 2

THE RECIPES

Variety is the spice of life, and a stroll through any Indian **market** proves how completely Indian **cooks** have taken this notion to heart. Cascading piles of delicate fresh cilantro, **sun-ripened** fruits and vegetables, and nuts and seeds of every shape, **texture**, and color abound. The air is a riot of **aromas**, some sweet, some spicy, others pungent or earthy. Sacks of **golden** turmeric and fiery ground chilies look like artists' color pigments, but Indian cooks **transform** them into another art form altogether—one that is surprisingly **accessible** and, as the recipes in this section show, **easy** to recreate in your own home.

Food occupies a central place in Indian life and meals are **social events** that bring family and friends **together**, whether for religious festivals, special occasions, or simply supper at the end of an ordinary day. From **cooling** yogurt relishes and **silky** dals to the sharp heat of chili-infused curries and the subtle **sweetness** of simple nut- and milk-based desserts, these mouthwatering recipes show you how to bring the **flavors** of India to life, to produce the best Indian meal you've ever **tasted**—and all made by you.

VEGETABLE SAMOSAS *SAMOSAS*

MAKES **16**   PREPARATION TIME: *20* MINUTES   COOKING TIME: *20* MINUTES

2 tablespoons **vegetable oil**, plus extra for deep-frying

½ teaspoon **cumin seeds**

2 **green chilies**, finely chopped

1 **onion**, chopped

¼ teaspoon **salt**

¼ teaspoon **ground coriander**

a pinch **Garam Masala** (*see page 23*)

1½ cups **potatoes**, roughly mashed

a handful **cilantro leaves**, chopped

1 recipe quantity **Samosa Pastry Dough** (*see page 30*)

¼ cup **all-purpose flour** mixed with a little water to make a "glue"

1 **HEAT** the oil in a saucepan over medium heat. Add the cumin seeds and fry, stirring, about 30 seconds, or until they splutter. Watch carefully so they do not burn. Add the chilies and onion and continue frying, stirring occasionally, 6 to 8 minutes until the onions are golden brown. Add the salt, ground coriander, and garam masala and continue stirring 1 minute. Stir in the mashed potato and cilantro leaves.

2 **DIVIDE** the dough into 8 balls of equal size and roll out on a lightly floured surface into thin 15-inch rounds, then cut each in half.

3 **APPLY** the "glue" to the straight edge of each semicircle. Fold the dough into a cone shape, sealing the pasted straight edge, then hold the cone with the tapered end down and fill it with about 1 tablespoon of the potato mixture.

4 **SEAL** the samosa with a little more "glue," pressing the edges firmly together. Repeat until all the dough and filling are used.

5 **HEAT** enough oil for deep-frying in a heavy-bottomed saucepan over high heat or in a deep-fat fryer to 375°F, or until a small piece of dough sizzles in the oil and comes to the surface.

6 **FRY** a few samosas at a time 3 to 4 minutes until golden brown, then remove with a slotted spoon and drain on paper towels. Continue frying the samosas in batches. Return the oil to the correct temperature before adding each new batch. Once fried, these keep in the refrigerator up to 2 days. Reheat in an oven at 350°F 10 to 15 minutes before serving. Refrigerate uncooked samosas up to 4 days, or freeze 1 month. Serve hot with Cilantro Chutney (see page 19).

ONION FRITTERS *PYAAZ PAKORAS*

MAKES 24   PREPARATION TIME: 10 MINUTES
COOKING TIME: 15 MINUTES

Pakoras *are batter-fried snacks usually eaten as an appetizer. The batter is made of spiced chickpea or gram flour and is used to coat vegetables or fish to create a variety of fritters. On Indian restaurant menus, you will also see pakoras listed as* bhajis *or* bhajias.

scant 1½ cups **chickpea** or **gram flour**

3 **onions**, sliced

1 teaspoon **cumin seeds**, crushed

1 teaspoon **coriander seeds**, crushed

¼ teaspoon **chili powder**

½ teaspoon **salt**

vegetable oil for deep-frying

1 **SIFT** the flour into a large bowl. Add the onions, cumin and coriander seeds, chili powder, and salt and stir together. Make a well in the middle, add ¼ cup water to the well, and then mix with a fork until the mixture forms a thick, stiff batter. If it appears runny, add extra flour.

2 **HEAT** enough oil for deep-frying in a heavy-bottomed saucepan over high heat or in a deep-fat fryer to 375°F, or until a small drop of the batter sizzles fiercely in the oil.

3 **DROP** 1 tablespoon of the batter into the oil and fry about 1 minute, or until it turns golden brown.

4 **REMOVE** the fritter from the oil with a slotted spoon and drain on paper towels. Taste the fritter and adjust the seasoning of the batter, adding more salt or chili powder, if necessary.

5 **FRY** the remaining fritters, working in batches to avoid overcrowding the pan, if necessary. Remove any pieces of fried batter from the oil and return the oil to the correct temperature before adding each new batch. These fritters can be fried in advance and reheated in an oven at 350°F 10 minutes before serving. Serve hot with Tomato Chutney (see page 21).

POTATO AND CILANTRO FRITTERS

ALOO BHAJIS

**MAKES 16 PREPARATION TIME: 10 MINUTES
COOKING TIME: 15 MINUTES**

The subtle heat of the green chilies, the nuttiness of the gram flour, and the cool, refreshing taste of cilantro make these fritters a delightful opening to a meal.

9 ounces **baking** or **Idaho potatoes**, peeled

heaped ⅓ cup **chickpea** or **gram flour**

2 **green chilies**, finely chopped

½ teaspoon **salt**

a handful **cilantro leaves**, finely chopped

vegetable oil for deep-frying

1 **GRATE** the potatoes coarsely into a large bowl.

2 **SIFT** the flour into the same bowl, then add the chilies, salt, and cilantro leaves. Stir together with a fork until the mixture forms a thick, coarse batter.

3 **HEAT** enough oil for deep-frying in a heavy-bottomed saucepan over a high heat or in a deep-fat fryer to 375°F, or until a small drop of the batter sizzles fiercely in the oil.

4 **DROP** 1 tablespoon of the batter into the oil and fry about 1 minute, or until it turns golden brown.

5 **REMOVE** the fritter from the oil with a slotted spoon and drain on paper towels. Taste the fritter and adjust the seasoning of the batter, adding more salt, if necessary.

6 **FRY** the remaining fritters, working in batches to avoid overcrowding the pan, if necessary. Remove any pieces of fried batter from the oil and return the oil to the correct temperature before adding each new batch. These fritters can be fried in advance and reheated in an oven at 350°F 10 minutes before serving. Serve hot with Tomato Chutney (see page 21).

CUMIN AND CORIANDER POTATO PATTIES

ALOO TIKKIYA

**MAKES 12   PREPARATION TIME: 30 MINUTES
COOKING TIME: 25 MINUTES**

In India, these snacks, also called bread cutlets, are sold as street food.

1½ cups peeled and chopped **baking or Idaho potatoes**

⅔ cup shelled **peas**, thawed if frozen

3 slices **white bread**

1 **onion**, finely chopped

½ teaspoon **ground coriander**

¼ teaspoon **salt**

¼ teaspoon **chili powder**

¼ teaspoon **ground cumin**

2-inch piece **gingerroot**, peeled and grated

a few **cilantro leaves**, finely chopped

¼ cup **vegetable oil**

1 **BRING** a pan of water to a boil over high heat. Add the potatoes and boil 15 minutes, or until tender, then drain well and set aside. Meanwhile, bring another pan of water to a boil. Add the peas and boil 8 to 10 minutes until tender, then drain well, mash, and set aside.

2 **SOAK** the bread in a bowl of cold water 5 minutes while the vegetables are boiling.

3 **PREHEAT** the oven to low.

4 **SQUEEZE** out as much of the water from the bread as possible. Place it in a bowl with the potatoes, peas, onion, ground coriander, salt, chili powder, cumin, ginger, and cilantro leaves and mix and mash together with a wooden spoon.

5 **WET** your hands slightly and roll the potato mixture into 12 balls of equal size, then flatten them until they are about ½ inch thick.

6 **HEAT** the oil in a skillet over medium heat. Add as many potato patties as will fit and fry them about 4 minutes, turning once, until golden brown and crisp on both sides. Remove the patties from the pan, drain well on paper towels, and keep them warm in the oven while you fry the remainder. These can be fried in advance and reheated in an oven at 350°F 10 minutes before serving. Serve hot.

VEGETABLE PATTIES *SABZI TIKKIYA*

MAKES 8   PREPARATION TIME: 20 MINUTES
COOKING TIME: 25 MINUTES

A tikki *is either chopped meat or vegetables with spices that are formed into a ball, pressed into a patty like a hamburger, and then pan-fried.* Tikkiya, *the plural of* tikki, *are also often called cutlets.*

⅔ cup peeled and chopped **baking**
   or **Idaho potatoes**

⅔ cup diced **carrots**

⅔ cup shelled **peas**, thawed if frozen

2 **green chilies**, finely chopped

1 teaspoon freshly squeezed **lemon juice**

½ teaspoon **salt**

2 tablespoons **rice flour**

about 2 tablespoons **vegetable oil**

1 **BRING** a pan of water to a boil over high heat. Add the potatoes and boil 15 minutes, or until very tender, then drain well and set aside. Meanwhile, bring another pan of water to a boil. Add the carrots and peas and boil 8 to 10 minutes until tender, then drain well and set aside.

2 **PREHEAT** the oven to low.

3 **MASH** the potatoes and vegetables. Put them all in a bowl with the chilies, lemon juice, and salt and mix until fairly smooth.

4 **PUT** the rice flour on a plate. Wet your hands slightly and roll the mashed potato mixture into 8 balls of equal size, then flatten them until they are about 1¼ inches thick. Coat them in the rice flour and set aside.

5 **HEAT** 2 tablespoons oil in a large skillet over medium heat. Add as many vegetable patties as will fit and fry them about 4 minutes, turning once, until golden brown and crisp on both sides. Remove the patties from the pan, drain well on paper towels, and keep them warm in the oven. Fry the remaining patties in the same way, adding a little extra oil to the pan, if necessary. These can be fried in advance and reheated in an oven at 350°F for 10 minutes before serving. Serve hot.

TOMATO SOUP

TAMATAR SHORBA

SERVES 4   PREPARATION TIME: 10 MINUTES
COOKING TIME: 25 MINUTES

*This North Indian soup, created by cooking tomatoes with whole spices,
is an aromatic recipe that's great in the winter as well as the summer.*

2 tablespoons **peanut oil,** plus extra
  for drizzling

9 **black peppercorns**

2 **bay leaves**

1 **cinnamon stick**

2 **garlic** cloves, chopped

1 **onion**, chopped

1¼ pounds **tomatoes**, chopped

2-inch piece **gingerroot**, peeled and grated

2 teaspoons **sugar**

½ teaspoon **salt**

a pinch **chili powder** (optional)

a pinch freshly ground **black pepper**

1 BRING 3⅔ cups water to a boil. Heat the oil in a large saucepan over medium heat. Add the peppercorns, bay leaves, and cinnamon and fry, stirring, 30 seconds, or until you can smell the aroma of the spices. Watch carefully so they do not burn.

2 ADD the garlic and onion and continue stirring 6 to 8 minutes until the onion is golden brown. Add the tomatoes and fry 4 to 6 minutes longer until they are soft.

3 POUR in the boiling water, stir, and return to a boil. Reduce the heat to low and simmer, uncovered, 5 minutes, stirring occasionally.

4 ADD the ginger, sugar, salt, and chili powder, if using, and simmer 5 minutes longer. Remove the cinnamon stick.

5 TRANSFER the soup to a blender and blend, then strain through a nylon strainer into the rinsed pan. Reheat gently and serve hot, drizzled with the extra peanut oil and sprinkled with the black pepper.

LENTIL SOUP *DAL SHORBA*

SERVES 4   PREPARATION TIME: 10 MINUTES
COOKING TIME: 25 MINUTES

Shorba (or shorva*) is the Hindi word for soup. This spicy broth is made with red lentils, although you could just as easily use yellow lentils. Red lentils make a quicker-cooking version of the soup and are easier to digest.*

---

heaped ½ cup **split red lentils**

2 **green chilies**

1 tablespoon **butter**

3 **black peppercorns**

1 **garlic** clove, chopped

½ teaspoon **salt**

a pinch **asafoetida**

1 **BRING** 2¾ cups water to a boil in a large saucepan over high heat. Add the lentils and return the water to a boil. Partially cover the pan, reduce the heat to low, and simmer, stirring occasionally, 15 minutes, or until the lentils become mushy. Watch carefully so the lentils don't burn. Top up with extra water, if necessary. Bring ½ cup water to a boil while the lentils finish simmering.

2 **CUT** off the chili stems and make a slit on each of the chilies; set aside.

3 **MELT** the butter in a small skillet over medium heat. Add the chilies, peppercorns, garlic, salt, and asafoetida. let the spices sizzle 30 seconds, or until you can smell the aroma. Watch carefully so they do not burn. Pour the mixture carefully into the lentils.

4 **POUR** the boiling water over and continue simmering, uncovered, 5 minutes, or until the spices have blended into the lentils. Serve hot.

TANDOORI CHICKEN BITES

MURGH TIKKA

MAKES **8**   PREPARATION TIME: **10** MINUTES, PLUS AT LEAST **2** HOURS
MARINATING TIME   COOKING TIME: **10** TO **15** MINUTES

In India, these would be cooked in a tandoor, *a clay oven with a rounded side and charcoal at the bottom. The meat prepared in a tandoor is generally moist and tender and has a special earthy aroma. In an ordinary domestic kitchen, however, these remain equally moist cooked in the oven, under a broiler, or on a barbecue.*

2-inch piece **gingerroot**, peeled and grated

4 **garlic** cloves, crushed

¼ cup **heavy cream**

2 tablespoons **vegetable oil**, plus extra
   for brushing the oven shelf or broiler rack

2 tablespoons **plain yogurt**

1 tablespoon **tomato paste**

1 teaspoon **Garam Masala** *(see page 23)*

1 tablespoon **paprika**

1 teaspoon **ground cumin**

½ teaspoon **salt**

½ teaspoon **chili powder**

18 ounces boneless, skinless **chicken breast**,
   chopped into bite-size pieces

1 MIX all the ingredients, except the chicken pieces, together in a large bowl. Add the chicken pieces and stir until they are well coated in the marinade.

2 COVER the bowl with cling film and refrigerate at least 2 hours, or overnight.

3 PREHEAT the oven to 350ºF or heat the broiler to medium.

4 SOAK 8 wooden skewers in cold water 15 minutes, while the oven is heating. Lightly grease the oven shelf or broiler rack.

5 THREAD the chicken onto the skewers, then place directly onto the oven shelves or under the broiler and cook, turning and brushing with oil at least once, 10 to 15 minutes, or until the chicken is cooked through. To check if the chicken is cooked, cut one piece—the juices should run clear. If not, cook for a few minutes more, then check again. Serve hot with Tomato, Onion, and Chili Salad (see page 160) and Cilantro Chutney (see page 19).

CHILI CHICKEN *MIRCH WALI MURGH*

SERVES 4   PREPARATION TIME: 10 MINUTES
COOKING TIME: 12 MINUTES

This spicy dish is a hybrid influenced by Chinese elements, and the piquant flavors of the soy sauce blend well with the sharpness of the turmeric and green chilies.

---

2 tablespoons **soy sauce**

1 tablespoon **tomato paste**

1 tablespoon **tomato sauce**

1 teaspoon **chili sauce**

1 teaspoon **malt vinegar** or **distilled white vinegar**

1 teaspoon **sugar**

¼ teaspoon freshly ground **black pepper**

1 pound boneless, skinless **chicken breast**, cut into strips

2 tablespoons **cornstarch**

½ teaspoon **turmeric**

¼ teaspoon **salt**

¼ cup **peanut** or **vegetable oil**

2 **garlic** cloves, chopped

1 **onion**, sliced, plus extra cut into rings, for serving

1 **green chili**, chopped, plus extra sliced, for serving

1 **STIR** the soy sauce, tomato paste, tomato sauce, chili sauce, vinegar, sugar, and black pepper together in a small bowl, then set aside.

2 **PUT** the chicken strips in a large bowl with the cornstarch, turmeric, and salt and mix well.

3 **HEAT** the oil in a large skillet or wok over a medium heat. Add the chicken pieces and fry, stirring occasionally, 5 minutes, or until they change color. Remove the chicken pieces from the pan with a slotted spoon and set aside.

4 **ADD** the garlic and onion to the oil remaining in the pan and fry, stirring, 3 minutes.

5 **ADD** the green chili and fry 1 minute. Return the chicken pieces to the pan and fry 1 minute longer.

6 **STIR** in the spicy sauce mixture and stir 2 minutes, or until the chicken pieces are cooked through. Check by cutting into a piece of chicken—the juices should run clear. Serve hot topped with the onion rings and sliced green chilies.

GROUND LAMB KEBABS *SEEKH KABOBS*

MAKES **12**   PREPARATION TIME: **10** MINUTES, PLUS AT LEAST **2** HOURS
MARINATING TIME   COOKING TIME: **10** TO **15** MINUTES

The seekh kabob *is one of the best-known tandoori dishes in Indian cooking. There are many recipes for these kebabs, and each cook adds his or her own ingredients to give it a special flavor. Below is one of the most basic recipes, which uses a paste made of fried onions for a typical northern Indian sweetness. These are also ideal for cooking over a barbecue.*

18 ounces **ground lamb**

2-inch piece **gingerroot**, peeled and grated

4 **green chilies**, finely chopped

1 teaspoon **Garam Masala** (*see page 23*)

1 teaspoon **paprika**

½ teaspoon **salt**

4 tablespoons **vegetable oil**, plus extra for brushing the broiler rack

2 **onions**, finely chopped

1 SOAK 12 wooden skewers in cold water 15 minutes. This prevents them from burning when they are heated.

2 PUT the lamb in a large bowl, add the ginger, chilies, garam masala, paprika, and salt and mix well.

3 HEAT the oil in a large skillet over a medium heat. Add the onions and fry, stirring occasionally, 8 to 10 minutes until they are caramelized. Watch carefully so they do not burn.

4 PREHEAT the broiler to high and lightly grease the broiler rack while the onions are frying.

5 ADD the onions to the lamb mixture and mix thoroughly.

6 DIVIDE the mixture into 12 equal portions. Wet your hands and shape each portion around a skewer, smoothing over the "seam."

7 PLACE the skewers under the broiler and broil 10 to 15 minutes, turning occasionally, until the meat is cooked through. These kebabs can be cooked in advance and warmed in an oven at 350°F 10 minutes before serving. Serve hot with Cucumber Relish (see page 22) and Tomato, Onion, and Chili Salad (see page 160).

DEEP-FRIED FISH *MACCHI AMRITSARI*

**MAKES ABOUT 24 PIECES   PREPARATION TIME: 10 MINUTES
COOKING TIME: 15 TO 20 MINUTES**

Amritsar, in Punjab in northern India, is steeped in history. These ajowan-laced fish fritters with a hint of chili are a snack from that region. Any white fish, such as cod, halibut, or coley, can be used to prepare them.

1 teaspoon **salt**

18 ounces skinless **haddock filets**, cut into bite-size pieces

¾ cup **chickpea** or **gram flour**

½ teaspoon **ground cumin**

½ teaspoon **ajowan seeds**

1-inch piece **gingerroot**, peeled and grated

2 **garlic** cloves, finely chopped

2 **green chilies**, finely chopped

1 tablespoon **malt vinegar** or **distilled white vinegar**

vegetable oil for deep-frying

1 SPRINKLE ½ teaspoon salt over the fish and set aside.

2 PUT the remaining salt, the chickpea or gram flour, cumin, and ajowan seeds in a large bowl and mix together. Stir in the ginger, garlic, and chilies, then add the vinegar and 6 tablespoons water to make a thick, coarse batter. Add the fish to the batter and gently stir to make sure all the pieces are coated but don't break up.

3 HEAT enough oil for deep-frying in a heavy-bottomed saucepan over high heat or in a deep-fat fryer to 375ºF, or until a small drop of batter sizzles fiercely in the oil. Place 1 piece of the fish in the oil and fry 2 minutes, or until it is golden brown. Remove the fish from the oil with a slotted spoon and drain on paper towels. Taste the fish and adjust the seasoning of the batter, adding more salt, if necessary.

4 FRY the remaining pieces of fish, working in batches to avoid overcrowding the pan, if necessary. Remove any pieces of fried batter from the oil and return the oil to the correct temperature before adding each new batch. These can be fried in advance and reheated in an oven at 350ºF 10 minutes before serving. Serve hot with Cilantro Chutney (see page 19).

SHRIMP FRITTERS *JHINGA PAKORAS*

MAKES **24**   PREPARATION TIME: **15** MINUTES
COOKING TIME: **15** TO **20** MINUTES

These are heavenly, golden, mini clusters of shrimp in a spicy, crispy batter.

¼ teaspoon **turmeric**

¼ teaspoon **salt**

9 ounces, shelled and cooked **shrimp**

1-inch piece **gingerroot**, peeled and finely chopped

4 **garlic** cloves, chopped

1 **onion**, finely chopped

¾ cup **chickpea** or **gram flour**

½ teaspoon **ground cumin**

¼ teaspoon **chili powder**

vegetable oil for deep-frying

1 SPRINKLE the turmeric and salt over the shrimp and set aside.

2 PUT the ginger, garlic, and onion in a large bowl, then stir in the flour, cumin, and chili powder.

3 POUR in 7 tablespoons water and mix with a fork until a thick batter forms. If it is runny, add a little extra flour, then stir in the shrimp.

4 HEAT enough oil for deep-frying in a heavy-bottomed saucepan over high heat or in a deep-fat fryer to 375º, or until a small drop of the batter sizzles fiercely in the oil.

5 DROP 1 tablespoon of the batter into the oil and fry 1 minute, or until it turns golden brown.

6 REMOVE the fritter from the oil with a slotted spoon and drain on paper towels. Let cool 1 minute, then taste the fritter and adjust the seasoning of the batter, adding more salt, if necessary.

7 FRY the remaining fritters, working in batches to avoid overcrowding the pan, if necessary. Remove any pieces of fried batter from the oil and return the oil to the correct temperature before adding each new batch. These can be fried in advance and reheated in an oven at 350ºF 10 minutes. Serve hot.

SHRIMP POORIS *JHINGA POORIS*

SERVES 4   PREPARATION TIME: 10 MINUTES, PLUS MAKING THE POORIS
COOKING TIME: 20 MINUTES

This spicy shrimp dish with deep-fried breads is very likely influenced by the foods of West Bengal and Bangladesh.

10 ounces shelled **jumbo shrimp**

¼ teaspoon **turmeric**

¼ teaspoon **salt**

3 tablespoons **peanut** or **vegetable oil**

1-inch piece **gingerroot**, peeled and chopped

2 **green chilies**, chopped

2 **garlic** cloves, chopped

1 **onion**, chopped

2 **tomatoes**, chopped

2 teaspoons **tomato paste**

2 teaspoons **sugar**

½ teaspoon **ground coriander**

½ teaspoon **ground cumin**

½ teaspoon **paprika**

1 teaspoon **distilled white vinegar**

1 recipe quantity **Pooris** (*see page 30*), cooked and reheated, to serve

1 PLACE the shrimp in a large bowl and sprinkle the turmeric and salt over, then set aside.

2 HEAT the oil in a saucepan or wok over medium heat. Add the ginger, chilies, garlic, and onion and fry, stirring frequently, 6 to 8 minutes until the onion is golden brown.

3 STIR in the tomatoes, tomato paste, sugar, coriander, cumin, and paprika. Reduce the heat to medium-low and simmer, stirring often, 5 minutes, or until the sauce turns dark red.

4 ADD the marinated shrimp and the vinegar and cook 3 minutes longer, or until the mixture becomes very thick and droplets of oil are visible on the surface. Serve the shrimp mixture hot, allowing 2 pooris per person. The pooris can be made several hours in advance and reheated in an oven at 350°F for 5 minutes before serving.

CHICKPEA CURRY *CHANNA MASALA*

**SERVES 4 PREPARATION TIME: 15 MINUTES
COOKING TIME: 25 MINUTES**

This spicy and tangy Punjabi recipe uses brewed tea to darken the sauce.

1 **black tea bag**

6 tablespoons **vegetable oil**

2 **bay leaves**

2- to 2½-inch piece **cassia bark** or **cinnamon stick**

2 **onions**, finely chopped

2-inch piece **gingerroot**, peeled and chopped

6 **garlic** cloves

1 teaspoon **ground cumin**

1 teaspoon **ground coriander**

½ teaspoon **turmeric**

½ teaspoon **salt**

¼ teaspoon **mango powder**

¼ teaspoon **chili powder**

¼ teaspoon **ground pomegranate seeds**

¼ teaspoon **Garam Masala** (*see page 23*)

2 cans (14 ounces each) **chickpeas**, drained and rinsed

1 **BRING** 2 cups water to a boil. Put the tea bag in a heatproof bowl, pour the boiling water over, and set aside to brew.

2 **HEAT** the oil in a large saucepan over medium heat. Add the bay leaves and the cassia bark or cinnamon and fry, stirring constantly, 30 seconds, or until they splutter. Watch carefully, so they do not burn.

3 **ADD** the onions and fry, stirring frequently, 6 to 8 minutes until they are golden brown.

4 **PUT** the ginger and garlic in a blender and blend until a coarse paste forms. Add to the pan with the cumin, coriander, turmeric, salt, mango powder, chili powder, ground pomegranate seeds, and garam masala and continue stirring 2 minutes.

5 **ADD** the chickpeas and continue stirring 5 minutes longer, mashing some of the chickpeas against the side of the pan with a wooden spoon.

6 **DISCARD** the tea bag, pour the tea into the pan, and simmer 7 to 8 minutes, stirring occasionally, until it becomes quite thick. Serve with Chapatis (see page 29) and Cilantro Chutney (see page 19).

FRIED LEGUMES *BHUNA DAL*

SERVES 4   PREPARATION TIME: 10 MINUTES, PLUS 1 HOUR SOAKING TIME
COOKING TIME: 30 TO 40 MINUTES

¼ cup **split yellow lentils**

¼ cup **split red lentils**

¼ cup **split dried mung beans**

¼ cup **split Bengal gram**

5 tablespoons **butter** or **ghee**

a pinch **asafoetida**

4 **garlic** cloves, finely chopped

1 **onion**, finely chopped

¼ teaspoon **salt**

¼ teaspoon **turmeric**

¼ teaspoon **chili powder**

¼ teaspoon **Garam Masala** (*see page 23*)

½ teaspoon **brown** or **black mustard seeds**

¼ teaspoon **cumin seeds**

2-inch piece **gingerroot**, peeled and grated

8 **curry leaves**

2 **green chilies**, chopped

1 PLACE the lentils, mung beans, and Bengal gram in a bowl, cover with cold water, and let soak 1 hour.

2 BRING 1¼ quarts water to a boil when the legumes have almost finished soaking. Drain the legumes, then place them in a large saucepan over high heat. Pour the boiling water over and return the water to a boil. Partially cover the pan, reduce the heat to low, and simmer, stirring occasionally, 20 to 30 minutes until yellow and mushy. Watch carefully so the legumes do not burn. Top up with extra water, if necessary.

3 MELT 3½ tablespoons of the butter or ghee in a separate pan over medium heat. Stir in the asafoetida, garlic, and onion and fry, stirring frequently, 6 to 8 minutes until the onion is golden brown. Stir in the salt, turmeric, and chili powder, then add the legumes with any remaining cooking water and simmer, uncovered, stirring occasionally, 10 minutes. Sprinkle with the garam masala.

4 MELT the remaining butter in a small skillet over medium heat. Add the mustard and cumin seeds and stir about 30 seconds until they begin to splutter. Watch carefully so they do not burn. Stir in the ginger, curry leaves, and chilies and stir a further 30 seconds.

5 POUR the spice mixture over the lentils. Serve hot.

KIDNEY BEANS IN SPICY TOMATO AND GARLIC SAUCE *RAJMAH LABABDAR*

SERVES 4 PREPARATION TIME: 15 MINUTES
COOKING TIME: 25 TO 30 MINUTES

Particularly popular in Kashmir and Punjab, this hearty dish tastes even better the day after it is made.

3 tablespoons **vegetable oil**

1 teaspoon **cumin seeds**

4 **garlic** cloves, chopped

1 **onion**, chopped

3 **tomatoes**, chopped

1-inch piece **gingerroot**, peeled and grated

¼ teaspoon **chili powder**

¼ teaspoon **ground ginger**

2 cans (14 ounces each) **red kidney beans**, drained and rinsed

1 tablespoon **butter**

¼ teaspoon **salt**

¼ teaspoon **Garam Masala** (*see page 23*)

a few **cilantro leaves**, roughly chopped

1 **HEAT** the oil in a large saucepan over medium heat. Add the cumin seeds and fry, stirring, 30 seconds, or until they splutter. Watch carefully so they do not burn.

2 **ADD** the garlic and onion and fry, stirring frequently, 6 to 8 minutes until the onion is golden brown. Bring 1½ cups water to a boil while the onion fries.

3 **ADD** the tomatoes to the pan and continue frying, stirring occasionally, 5 minutes. Add the gingerroot, chili powder, and ground ginger and continue stirring 1 minute longer. Stir in the kidney beans.

4 **POUR** half the boiling water over and add the butter. Use a wooden spoon to mash a few of the beans against the side of the pan, then simmer 4 to 5 minutes. Add the remaining boiling water and continue simmering, uncovered, 7 minutes, stirring occasionally, until the mixture thickens.

5 **STIR** in the salt and garam masala and serve hot, sprinkled with the cilantro leaves.

VEGETABLE DHANSAK *PARSI DHANSAK*

SERVES 4   PREPARATION TIME: 10 MINUTES
COOKING TIME: 50 TO 55 MINUTES

A dhansak is a spiced dish of pureed lentils and vegetables cooked in a tangy sauce. This is a Parsi recipe from western India.

½ cup **split yellow lentils**

½ cup **split dried yellow mung beans**

1½ cups peeled and quartered **baking** or **Idaho potatoes**

heaped 1 cup chopped **carrots**

½ cup **butter** or **ghee**

2-inch piece **gingerroot**, peeled and chopped

4 **garlic** cloves, chopped

3 **green chilies**, chopped

2 **onions**, chopped

1 tablespoon **Dhansak Masala** (*see page 24*)

½ teaspoon **turmeric**

½ teaspoon **salt**

2 **tomatoes**, finely chopped

1 BRING 3⅓ cups water to a boil over a high heat. Add the lentils and mung beans and return the water to a boil. Partially cover the pan, reduce the heat to low, and simmer, stirring occasionally, 35 to 40 minutes until the mixture becomes mushy. Watch carefully so the mixture does not burn. Top up with extra boiling water, if necessary.

2 BRING another large saucepan of water to a boil over high heat while the lentils are simmering. Add the potatoes and carrots return the water to a boil, and boil 20 to 25 minutes until both vegetables are very tender and the potatoes are almost falling apart, then drain well.

3 POUR the lentils and any remaining water into a blender. Add the drained potatoes and carrots and blend until the mixture forms a thick puree; set aside.

4 MELT the butter or ghee in a large saucepan over medium-low heat. Add the ginger, garlic, chilies, and onions and fry, stirring occasionally, 10 minutes, or until the onions are caramelized.

5 STIR in the dhansak masala, turmeric, and salt, then add the tomatoes and cook 1 minute, stirring occasionally. Stir in the lentil and vegetable mixture and continue stirring 2 minutes, then serve.

BUTTERY SPINACH AND POTATOES

SAAG ALOO

SERVES 4   PREPARATION TIME: 15 MINUTES
COOKING TIME: 25 MINUTES

This popular vegetarian dish, served in Indian restaurants around the world, can be made with spinach or mustard leaves. If the fresh spinach in this recipe is unavailable or out of season, replace it with frozen chopped spinach, thawed before you add it to the pan.

4 tablespoons **butter** or **ghee**

2-inch piece **gingerroot**, peeled and grated

4 **garlic** cloves, chopped

2 **onions**, chopped

2 **green chilies**, chopped

7 ounces **baking potatoes**, peeled and cut into 2-inch cubes (about 1⅓ cups)

1 teaspoon **ground cumin**

1 teaspoon **ground coriander**

½ teaspoon **turmeric**

¼ teaspoon **salt**

18 ounces rinsed and chopped **spinach leaves** (about 9 cups)

a pinch **Garam Masala** (*see page 23*)

1 MELT the butter or ghee in a large saucepan over medium heat. Add the ginger, garlic, onions, and chilies and fry, stirring frequently, 2 minutes.

2 ADD the potatoes and continue stirring 5 minutes.

3 STIR in the cumin, coriander, turmeric, and salt, followed by the spinach with just the water clinging to the leaves and continue frying and stirring 15 minutes, or until the potatoes are tender.

4 SPRINKLE the garam masala over and serve hot with Chickpea Curry (see page 62) and Chapatis (see page 29).

POTATOES WITH CAULIFLOWER

ALOO GOBHI MASALA

SERVES 4   PREPARATION TIME: 15 MINUTES
COOKING TIME: 25 MINUTES

In India, cauliflower is harvested during the winter months. The nation ranks second in the production of this vegetable, so this recipe is extremely popular. It is usually featured in dishes that contain little sauce and is often served alongside a lentil dish.

¼ cup **vegetable oil**

1 teaspoon **brown mustard seeds**

1¼ pounds **waxy potatoes**, peeled and cut into 1-inch pieces (about 4 cups)

1-inch piece **gingerroot**, peeled and chopped

4 **garlic** cloves, chopped

2 **green chilies**, chopped

1 **onion**, chopped

1 teaspoon **turmeric**

1 teaspoon **ground cumin**

½ teaspoon **salt**

1¼ pounds **cauliflower** florets (about 4 cups)

¼ teaspoon **Garam Masala** (*see page 23*)

a few **cilantro leaves**, roughly chopped

1 HEAT the oil in a saucepan over medium heat. Add the mustard seeds and stir 30 seconds, or until the seeds start to splutter. Watch carefully so they do not burn.

2 ADD the potatoes, increase the heat to medium-high, and continue stirring 6 minutes, or until the edges brown. Bring 1¼ cups water to a boil while the potatoes cook.

3 ADD the ginger, garlic, chilies, and onion to the potatoes and continue frying, stirring frequently, 5 minutes. Add the turmeric, ground cumin, and salt, followed by the cauliflower. Continue frying, stirring occasionally, 3 minutes. Pour in the boiling water and stir well.

4 COVER the pan and simmer 9 to 10 minutes until the potatoes and cauliflower are tender.

5 STIR in the garam masala and sprinkle with the cilantro. Serve hot with Chapatis (see page 29).

SWEET POTATO CURRY

SHAKARKAND KI CURRY

**SERVES 4   PREPARATION TIME: 10 MINUTES
COOKING TIME: 15 MINUTES**

Many Hindus in India eat sweet potatoes during religious festivals in the summer when the tubers are simply baked or boiled. At other times they are used in more flavorsome dishes such as this one.

1 ¼ pounds **sweet potatoes**, peeled and cut into bite-size chunks (about 4 cups)

½ teaspoon **salt**

2 tablespoons **vegetable oil**

1 **green chili**, chopped

½ teaspoon **cumin seeds**

a few chopped **cilantro leaves**

1 BRING 2½ cups water to a boil in a large saucepan over high heat. Add the sweet potatoes and ¼ teaspoon of the salt and return the water to a boil, then reduce the heat and simmer 10 minutes, or until the sweet potatoes are tender when pierced with the tip of a knife.

2 DRAIN the sweet potatoes well, carefully shaking off any excess water, then set aside.

3 HEAT the oil in a large skillet or wok over a medium heat. Add the chili and cumin seeds and fry 30 seconds, stirring, or until the seeds splutter. Watch carefully so the spices do not burn.

4 ADD the sweet potatoes and the remaining ¼ teaspoon salt and stir 2 minutes until well combined and the sweet potatoes are hot.

5 SPRINKLE with the cilantro leaves and serve hot.

MIXED VEGETABLE CURRY

HARA MASALA SABZI

**SERVES 4   PREPARATION TIME: 10 MINUTES
COOKING TIME: 20 MINUTES**

Vegetables have always been an extremely important part of the diet of all Indians, and many Indians are strict vegetarians for religious reasons.

2 **carrots**, cut into batons

⅔ cup shelled **peas**, thawed if frozen

⅔ cup **corn kernels**, thawed if frozen

1½ cups **broccoli** florets

1 **red bell pepper**, seeded and cut into chunks

3 tablespoons **vegetable oil**

1 recipe quantity **Green Masala Paste**
   (*see page 25*)

¼ teaspoon **salt**

1 BRING 2 cups water to a boil in a large saucepan over high heat. Add the carrots, peas, and corn kernels and boil 5 minutes. Add the broccoli and red pepper and continue boiling 5 minutes longer. Drain the vegetables and set aside.

2 HEAT the oil in a large saucepan or wok over medium heat while the vegetables are cooking. Add the green masala paste and salt and fry, stirring constantly, 3 minutes. Watch carefully so the mixture does not brown too much.

3 ADD the vegetables to the pan and stir. Continue frying, stirring to combine the ingredients, 3 minutes. Bring 1¼ cups water to a boil while the vegetables are frying.

4 POUR the boiling water over and continue simmering 1 minute longer, or until droplets of oil appear on the surface. Serve hot with Plain Basmati Rice (see page 31).

PANEER WITH PEAS

MATTAR PANEER

**SERVES 4 PREPARATION TIME: 10 MINUTES
COOKING TIME: 20 TO 25 MINUTES**

This dish is eaten all over northern India, practically on a daily basis.

---

3 **tomatoes**, roughly chopped

5 tablespoons **vegetable oil**

18 ounces **paneer**, cut into bite-size cubes

2 teaspoon **cumin seeds**

1-inch piece **gingerroot**, peeled and chopped

6 **garlic** cloves, chopped

2 **onions**, chopped

¼ teaspoon **turmeric**

¼ teaspoon **chili powder**

½ teaspoon **salt**

1⅔ cups shelled **peas**, defrosted if frozen

¼ teaspoon **Garam Masala** (*see page 23*)

3 tablespoons **heavy cream**

a few **cilantro leaves**, roughly chopped

1 PUT the tomatoes and their juice into a blender and blend until smooth, then set aside.

2 HEAT the oil in a wok or saucepan over medium heat. Add the paneer and fry about 4 minutes, gently turning occasionally, until the edges are browned; remove with a slotted spoon and set aside.

3 ADD the cumin seeds to the oil remaining in the pan and fry, stirring constantly, 30 seconds, or until the seeds splutter. Watch carefully so they do not burn. Add the ginger, garlic, and onions and fry, stirring frequently, 6 to 8 minutes until the onions are golden brown, then stir in the turmeric, chili powder, and salt. Bring 1¼ cups water to a boil, while the onions are frying.

4 ADD the peas to the pan and continue stirring 2 minutes. Add the blended tomatoes and simmer 3 minutes longer.

5 RETURN the paneer to the pan and add the boiling water. Stir well and simmer, uncovered, 5 minutes, or until droplets of oil appear on the surface.

6 SPRINKLE with the garam masala, swirl in the cream, and scatter the cilantro leaves over. Serve hot.

REGAL PANEER *SHAHI PANEER*

SERVES 4   PREPARATION TIME: 15 MINUTES   COOKING TIME: 15 MINUTES

The Moghul influence of using dairy products in cooking is obvious in dishes like this from Hyderabad. This is a deliciously piquant, hot, and creamy curry.

1 large **plum tomato**, coarsely chopped

1 tablespoon **cornstarch**

3 tablespoons **vegetable oil**

2 **black cardamom pods**

1 teaspoon **cumin seeds**

4 **garlic** cloves, crushed

2 **green chilies**, finely chopped

1 **onion**, finely chopped

2 tablespoons **plain yogurt**, whisked

1 tablespoon **tomato paste**

1 teaspoon **sugar**

½ teaspoon **salt**

a pinch **chili powder**

18 ounces **paneer**, cut into bite-size cubes

2-inch piece **gingerroot**, peeled and grated

2 tablespoons **heavy cream**

a pinch **Garam Masala** (*see page 23*)

a few **cilantro leaves**

1 PUT the tomatoes and their juice into a blender and blend until smooth, then set aside. Put the cornstarch in a small bowl and stir in 2 tablespoons water to make a smooth paste, then set aside.

2 HEAT the oil in a large saucepan over medium heat. Add the cardamom pods and cumin seeds and fry 30 seconds, stirring constantly, or until they splutter. Watch carefully so they do not burn.

3 ADD the garlic, chilies, and onion and continue frying, stirring frequently, 6 to 8 minutes until the onion turns golden brown.

4 ADD the tomatoes and simmer, uncovered, 4 minutes, or until the sauce thickens.

5 STIR in the yogurt, then the cornstarch paste. Add the tomato paste, sugar, salt, chili powder, and ¼ cup cold water and bring to a boil, stirring.

6 REDUCE the heat to low. Add the paneer and gently stir it into the sauce, then simmer, uncovered, 2 to 3 minutes until droplets of oil appear on the surface. Stir in the ginger.

7 SWIRL in the cream and sprinkle with the garam masala. Tear the cilantro leaves and scatter them over the paneer, then serve.

VEGETABLE BIRYANI *SABZ BIRYANI*

SERVES 4   PREPARATION TIME: 20 MINUTES   COOKING TIME: 40 MINUTES

5 tablespoons **butter**, plus extra for greasing

1 **onion**, sliced

2 x 2 inch pieces **cassia bark**

6 **green cardamom pods**

4 **cloves**

2 **bay leaves**

1 teaspoon **cumin seeds**

2 **carrots**, cut into batons

⅔ cup shelled **peas**, thawed if frozen

⅔ cup **corn kernels**, thawed if frozen

1½ cups **broccoli** florets

1 **red bell pepper**, cut into chunks

8 **cashew nuts**

1 cup **plain yogurt**, whisked

6 **garlic** cloves

½ teaspoon **Garam Masala** (*see page 23*)

½ teaspoon **chili powder**

½ teaspoon **salt**

1 recipe quantity **Plain Basmati Rice**
    (*see page 31*) , cooked

10 **saffron strands**

1 MELT the butter in a large saucepan over medium heat. Add the onion and fry, stirring occasionally, 6 to 8 minutes until it is golden brown. Remove the onion from the pan and set aside.

2 INCREASE the heat to medium-high. Add the cassia bark, green cardamom, cloves, bay leaves, and cumin seeds to the butter left in the pan and fry 30 seconds, stirring, or until you can smell the aroma.

3 ADD the vegetables and cashew nuts and continue frying 5 minutes, stirring occasionally, or until the nuts are golden brown.

4 PREHEAT the oven to 350°F. Grease a large baking dish with a tight-fitting lid.

5 PUT the onion in a blender. Add the yogurt, garlic, garam masala, chili powder, and salt and blend until smooth. Stir this mixture into the vegetables.

6 PLACE a layer of vegetables on the bottom of the dish and cover it with a layer of the cooked rice and a few saffron strands.

7 REPEAT these layers until all the ingredients are used, ending with a layer of rice. Cover and bake 25 minutes, or until the biryani is heated through. Serve hot with Cucumber Relish (see page 22).

CHICKEN TIKKA MASALA

MURGH TIKKA MASALA

SERVES 4   PREPARATION TIME: 15 MINUTES, PLUS AT LEAST 2 HOURS
MARINATING TIME   COOKING TIME: 15 TO 20 MINUTES

Now said to be the world's most popular Indian dish, this actually originated from the kitchens of Bangladeshi chefs in England.

4 **tomatoes**, chopped

6 tablespoons **heavy cream**

2-inch piece **gingerroot**, peeled and grated

4 **garlic** cloves, chopped

3 tablespoons **vegetable oil**

2 **bay leaves**

2 **onions**, finely chopped

2 **green chilies**, finely chopped

1 teaspoon **ground cumin**

1 teaspoon **ground coriander**

½ teaspoon **paprika**

¼ teaspoon **turmeric**

¼ teaspoon **salt**

a pinch **Garam Masala** (*see page 23*)

1 recipe quantity **Tandoori Chicken Bites**
    (*see page 51*), cooked

1 PLACE the tomatoes, cream, ginger, and garlic in a blender and blend until a thick sauce forms, then set aside.

2 HEAT the oil in a large saucepan with a tight-fitting lid over medium heat. Add the bay leaves and onions and fry, stirring constantly, 6 to 8 minutes until the onions are golden brown.

3 ADD the chilies, cumin, coriander, paprika, turmeric, salt, and garam masala and stir 1 minute, or until you can smell the aroma of the spices. Watch carefully so the mixture does not burn.

4 ADD the chicken pieces and fry, stirring occasionally, 3 minutes. Stir the tomato and cream mixture into the pan, cover, and reduce the heat to low. Simmer 5 minutes until the chicken is heated through.

5 BRING ½ cup water to a boil while the chicken mixture is simmering. Add boiling water to the chicken and simmer 1 minute longer, stirring, or until droplets of oil appear on the surface. Serve hot with Buttery Spinach and Potatoes (see page 70) and Plain Basmati Rice (see page 31).

CHICKEN BREAST MARINATED IN PICKLING SPICES *ACHAARI MURGH*

**SERVES 4   PREPARATION TIME: 10 MINUTES
COOKING TIME: 25 TO 30 MINUTES**

This North Indian dish is prepared with many of the whole spices traditionally used to make pickles. Mustard oil is often used in this spicy curry to give it a headier flavor, but milder-tasting vegetable oil is used here.

¼ cup **vegetable oil**

4 **dried red chilies**

½ teaspoon **brown mustard seeds**

½ teaspoon **fenugreek seeds**

½ teaspoon **cumin seeds**

½ teaspoon **nigella seeds**

½ teaspoon **fennel seeds**

2 **onions**, chopped

2-inch piece **gingerroot**, peeled and grated

6 **garlic** cloves, finely chopped

½ teaspoon **turmeric**

18 ounces boneless, skinless **chicken breast**, chopped into bite-size pieces

heaped 1 cup **plain yogurt**, whisked

1 teaspoon freshly squeezed **lemon juice**

1 **HEAT** the oil in a saucepan with a tight-fitting lid over medium-high heat. Add the chilies and the mustard, fenugreek, cumin, nigella, and fennel seeds and fry, stirring constantly, 30 seconds, or until the seeds splutter. Watch carefully so they do not burn.

2 **ADD** the onions and fry, stirring, 6 to 8 minutes until they are golden brown. Stir in the ginger, garlic, and turmeric.

3 **ADD** the chicken pieces and continue frying 8 to 10 minutes longer until the chicken colors on the outside. Bring ¾ cup water to a boil while the chicken cooks.

4 **STIR** in the yogurt, followed by the boiling water. Cover the pan, reduce the heat to low, and simmer 5 minutes, or until the chicken is cooked through. Check by cutting a piece of chicken in half—the juices should run clear.

5 **SPRINKLE** the lemon juice over and simmer 2 minutes longer, or until droplets of oil appear on the surface. Serve hot.

BUTTER CHICKEN *MURGH MAKHANI*

SERVES 4   PREPARATION TIME: 20 MINUTES, PLUS AT LEAST 30 MINUTES
MARINATING TIME   COOKING TIME: 20 TO 25 MINUTES

1 small **plum tomato,** peeled (*see page 18*)

4 **garlic** cloves, crushed

2 tablespoons **plain yogurt**

2 tablespoons **heavy cream**

½ teaspoon freshly ground **black pepper**

½ teaspoon **paprika**

¼ teaspoon **chili powder**

a large pinch **ground cinnamon**

¼ cup **vegetable oil**

18 ounces boneless, skinless **chicken breast,** cut into bite-sized pieces

2 **onions,** finely chopped

¼ teaspoon **salt**

¼ teaspoon **ground fenugreek**

1 tablespoon **butter**

¼ teaspoon **Garam Masala** (*see page 23*)

a few **cilantro leaves**

1 **PUT** the tomato into a blender and blend until smooth, then set aside.

2 **PUT** the garlic, yogurt, cream, black pepper, paprika, chili powder, cinnamon, and 1 tablespoon of the oil in a large bowl and stir well. Add the chicken pieces to this marinade and stir until well coated. Cover the bowl with plastic wrap and refrigerate at least 30 minutes, or overnight, to let the flavors blend.

3 **HEAT** the remaining 3 tablespoons oil in a large saucepan or wok over medium heat. Add the onions and fry, stirring occasionally, 6 to 8 minutes until golden brown. Add the salt and fenugreek and continue frying 1 minute longer until you can smell the aroma.

4 **ADD** the tomatoes and continue stirring 3 minutes, or until the mixture becomes very thick.

5 **STIR** in the butter, add the chicken and the marinade, reduce the heat to low, and simmer, uncovered, 10 minutes, stirring occasionally, or until the chicken is cooked through. Check by cutting a piece of chicken in half—the juices should run clear. Sprinkle the garam masala and cilantro leaves over and serve hot with Naans (see page 26).

CHICKEN DHANSAK *MURGH DHANSAK*

SERVES 4   PREPARATION TIME: 10 MINUTES, PLUS BOILING THE POTATOES AND CARROTS   COOKING TIME: 1 HOUR 20 MINUTES

½ cup **split Bengal gram**

1 cup trimmed and chopped **green beans**

1 cup peeled and chopped **carrots**

6 tablespoons **butter** or **ghee**

2-inch piece **gingerroot**, chopped

4 **garlic** cloves, chopped

3 **green chilies**, chopped

2 **onions**, chopped

4 teaspoons **Dhansak Masala** (*see page 24*)

½ teaspoon **turmeric**

½ teaspoon **salt**

18 ounces boneless, skinless **chicken breast**, cut into bite-size pieces

2 teaspoons **tomato paste**

1 BRING 1¾ cups water to a boil over high heat. Add the Bengal gram and return the water to a boil. Partially cover the pan, reduce the heat to low, and simmer, stirring occasionally, 55 minutes, or until the mixture becomes mushy. Watch carefully so it does not burn. Top up with extra boiling water, if necessary.

2 BRING another large saucepan of water to a boil over high heat while the Bengal gram is simmering. Add the green beans and carrots and boil 10 to 15 minutes until they are both soft, then drain well.

3 POUR the Bengal gram and any remaining water into a blender. Add the green beans and carrots and blend until smooth, then set aside.

4 MELT the butter or ghee in a large saucepan over medium heat. Add the ginger, garlic, chilies, and onions and fry, stirring frequently, 6 to 8 minutes until the onions are golden brown. Add the dhansak masala, turmeric, and salt to the onions and stir 30 seconds.

5 ADD the chicken to the pan with the onions and continue cooking, stirring, 5 minutes, or until the chicken changes color. Bring 1¼ cups water to a boil. Add the boiling water to the chicken, stir in the tomato paste, and simmer 1 minute longer, stirring.

6 STIR in the Bengal gram and vegetable mixture and simmer 5 to 7 minutes, stirring occasionally, until the chicken is cooked through. Check by cutting a piece of chicken in half—the juices should run clear. Serve hot.

CHICKEN WITH CARAMELIZED ONION, GARLIC, AND GINGER

MURGH MASALA

SERVES 4 PREPARATION TIME: 10 MINUTES
COOKING TIME: 25 TO 30 MINUTES

Onions, garlic, ginger, chili, and tomato form the foundation of many curries.

4 **tomatoes**, coarsely chopped

7 tablespoons **butter** or **ghee**

2-inch piece **cinnamon stick**

4 **cloves**

2 **onions**, finely chopped

4 **garlic** cloves, chopped

1 teaspoon **ground cumin**

1 teaspoon **ground coriander**

¼ teaspoon **turmeric**

¼ teaspoon **chili powder**

¼ teaspoon **salt**

18 ounces boneless, skinless **chicken breast**, cut into bite-size pieces

2-inch piece **gingerroot**, peeled and grated

¼ teaspoon **Garam Masala** (*see page 23*)

1 PUT the tomatoes into a blender and blend until smooth; set aside.

2 MELT the butter or ghee in a saucepan or wok over medium heat. Add the cinnamon and cloves and fry, stirring, 30 seconds, or until you can smell the aroma of the spices. Watch carefully so they do not burn.

3 ADD the onions and garlic and fry, stirring frequently, 6 to 8 minutes until they are golden brown. Add the cumin, coriander, turmeric, chili powder, and salt and stir 1 minute.

4 STIR in the chicken and continue frying, stirring, 7 to 8 minutes until the chicken colors. Bring 6½ tablespoons water to the boil while the chicken is cooking.

5 ADD the tomatoes, followed by the boiling water, to the chicken and simmer 10 to 15 minutes longer until droplets of oil appear on the surface.

6 STIR in the ginger and garam masala, then serve hot with Cucumber Relish (see page 22) and Chapatis (see page 29).

GRIDDLED CHICKEN *MURGH TAKA TAK*

SERVES 4   PREPARATION TIME: 10 MINUTES
COOKING TIME: 15 MINUTES

*This dish gets its Indian name from the sound of the spoon or spatula hitting the pan and breaking up the food while it cooks—*taka tak *is the rhythm of chopping the chicken pieces as they cook in the pan over high heat.*

¼ cup **vegetable oil**

1 teaspoon **cumin seeds**

2 **onions**, sliced

1-inch piece **gingerroot**, peeled and grated

6 **garlic** cloves, crushed

3 **green chilies**, chopped

18 ounces boneless, skinless **chicken breast**, cut into bite-size pieces

2 **tomatoes**, chopped

½ teaspoon **salt**

¼ teaspoon **turmeric**

a pinch **Garam Masala** (*see page 23*)

a handful **fenugreek leaves**

1 **HEAT** the oil in a large skillet or wok over medium heat. Add the cumin seeds and fry, stirring constantly, 30 seconds, or until they splutter. Watch carefully so they do not burn. Add the onions and continue frying, stirring, 3 minutes until they start to soften.

2 **ADD** the ginger, garlic, and chilies and continue frying 2 minutes, or until all the spices are blended.

3 **ADD** the chicken and fry 4 minutes, breaking the chicken into smaller pieces against the side of the pan with a wooden spoon or spatula, until the chicken changes color.

4 **ADD** the tomatoes, salt, turmeric, and garam masala and continue frying, stirring, 4 minutes.

5 **STIR** in the fenugreek leaves and fry 5 minutes longer until all the chicken pieces are cooked through. Check by cutting a piece of chicken in half—the juices should run clear. Serve hot with Cucumber Relish (see page 22) and Naans (see page 26).

CHICKEN JALFREZI *MURGH JALFREZI*

SERVES 4   PREPARATION TIME: 10 MINUTES
COOKING TIME: 20 TO 25 MINUTES

Jalfrezi is a dish in which meat or vegetables are fried in oil and spices to produce a thick, dry sauce. Peppers, onions, and fresh green chilies are then added to make a medium-hot curry.

3 tablespoons **vegetable oil**

2 **onions**, chopped

4 **garlic** cloves, sliced

2 **green chilies**, chopped

4 teaspoons **Manju's Quick Curry Paste**
(*see page 24*)

1 teaspoon **tomato paste**

¼ teaspoon **salt**

18 ounces, skinless **chicken breast**,
chopped into bite-size pieces

2-inch piece **gingerroot**, peeled and grated

2 **green bell peppers**, seeded and sliced

1 HEAT the oil in a large saucepan over a medium heat. Add the onions, garlic, and chilies and fry, stirring frequently, 6 to 8 minutes until the onions are golden brown.

2 ADD the curry paste, tomato paste, and salt and stir 1 minute. Stir in the chicken pieces and continue stirring 7 to 8 minutes until they change color and the spices blend with the chicken.

3 BRING 1 cup water to a boil and stir this into the pan.

4 ADD the ginger and green peppers and simmer, uncovered, 5 minutes, stirring occasionally, until the sauce thickens and the chicken is cooked through. Check by cutting a piece of chicken in half—the juices should run clear. Serve hot with Naans (see page 26).

CREAMY CHICKEN CURRY

KASHMIRI KORMA

SERVES **4** PREPARATION TIME: **10** MINUTES
COOKING TIME: **20** TO **25** MINUTES

Korma *just means a mild curry. Yet, it is actually a rich stew in which the meat, chicken, or vegetables and nuts are braised in cream, yogurt, or coconut milk.*

¼ cup **vegetable oil**

3 **garlic** cloves

2 **onions**, finely chopped

2 **green chilies**, finely chopped

1 teaspoon **ground cumin**

1 teaspoon **ground coriander**

½ teaspoon **turmeric**

¼ teaspoon **salt**

4 **green cardamom pods**, slightly crushed

2 teaspoons **tomato paste**

18 ounces boneless, skinless **chicken breast**, cut into bite-size pieces

1 cup **coconut milk**

20 **cashew nuts**, ground

2-inch piece **gingerroot**, peeled and grated

a generous pinch **Garam Masala** (*see page 23*)

1 **HEAT** the oil in a large saucepan or wok over medium heat. Add the garlic, onions, and chilies and fry, stirring frequently, 6 to 8 minutes until the onions turn golden brown.

2 **STIR** in the cumin, coriander, turmeric, salt, and cardamom pods and fry 1 minute, then stir in the tomato paste.

3 **ADD** the chicken pieces, reduce the heat to low, and fry, stirring, 7 to 8 minutes, or until they change color. Meanwhile, bring 1 cup water to a boil.

4 **ADD** the water and the coconut milk to the chicken, then add the ground nuts. Simmer, uncovered, stirring occasionally, 7 minutes, or until the chicken is cooked through. Check by cutting a piece of chicken in half—the juices should run clear.

5 **STIR** in the ginger and sprinkle the garam masala over. Serve hot.

HYDERABADI-STYLE LAMB

HYDERABADI GOSHT

**SERVES 4   PREPARATION TIME: 15 MINUTES
COOKING TIME: 1 HOUR 15 MINUTES**

Hyderabad, the capital city of Andhra Pradesh, has a strong fusion of Islamic culture and southern Indian traditions, which are reflected in its cuisine.

---

5 tablespoons **butter** or **ghee**

2-inch piece **gingerroot**, peeled and chopped

2 **onions**, sliced

7 **black peppercorns**

7 **garlic** cloves, chopped

5 **cloves**

4 **green cardamom pods**

3 **dried red chilies**, chopped in half

2 **cinnamon sticks**

18 ounces boneless **stewing lamb**, chopped

1¾ cups **plain yogurt**, whisked

16 **cashew nuts**, ground

1 teaspoon **turmeric**

1 teaspoon **cornstarch**

½ teaspoon **salt**

1 MELT the butter or ghee in a flameproof casserole with a tight-fitting lid over medium heat. Add the ginger, onions, peppercorns, garlic, cloves, cardamom pods, chilies, and cinnamon sticks and fry, stirring frequently, 5 minutes until the onions start to soften and you can smell the aroma of the spices. Watch carefully so the spices do not burn.

2 ADD the lamb and continue frying, stirring, 10 minutes, or until it looks brown. Bring 2½ cups water to a boil while the lamb is cooking.

3 POUR the boiling water into the pan and return to the boil, stirring once or twice. Cover the pan, reduce the heat to low, and simmer 55 minutes to 1 hour until the meat is tender.

4 MIX the yogurt, cashew nuts, turmeric, cornstarch, and salt in a bowl, then stir into the lamb mixture and simmer, uncovered, 3 minutes. Bring ½ cup water to a boil and stir into the lamb. Simmer 2 minutes longer, or until droplets of oil appear on the surface. Serve with Pulao Rice with Peas (see page 32) and Mint and Yogurt Chutney (see page 19).

LAMB MEATBALLS *MALAI KOFTA*

**MAKES 16 PREPARATION TIME: 20 MINUTES
COOKING TIME: 25 MINUTES**

In their simplest form, koftas *are meatballs flavored with spices.
However, in northern Indian cuisine, they are often cooked in a spicy
aromatic sauce with a rich garnish of nuts and cream.*

18 ounces **ground lamb**

2-inch piece **gingerroot**, peeled and grated

2 **green chilies**, chopped

2 **garlic** cloves, crushed

1 teaspoon **paprika**

1 teaspoon **salt**

3 tablespoons **vegetable oil**

2 **onions**, finely chopped

½ teaspoon **ground cumin**

½ teaspoon **ground coriander**

½ teaspoon **turmeric**

½ teaspoon **chili powder**

½ teaspoon **Garam Masala** (*see page 23*)

1 teaspoon **tomato paste**

2 tablespoons **heavy cream**

a handful **sliced almonds**

1 PUT the lamb in a large bowl and use your hands to mix in the ginger, chilies, garlic, paprika, and ⅓ teaspoon of the salt. Wet your hands and roll the mixture into 16 meatballs of equal size.

2 HEAT 3 tablespoons oil in a large skillet over medium-high heat. Add the meatballs and fry 6 to 7 minutes, turning them in the oil until they are light brown. It might be necessary to do this in batches, depending on the size of your pan. Add extra oil to the pan, if necessary. Use a slotted spoon to remove the meatballs from the pan and set aside.

3 ADD onions into the oil remaining in the pan and fry, stirring frequently, 6 to 8 minutes until they are golden brown. Bring 2 cups water to a boil while the onions are frying.

4 ADD the cumin, coriander, turmeric, chili powder, garam masala, and remaining ½ teaspoon salt. Fry, stirring occasionally, 1 minute until you can smell the aroma of the spices. Stir in the tomato paste.

5 RETURN the meatballs to the pan and pour in the boiling water. Reduce the heat to low, cover, and simmer 6 to 8 minutes until small droplets of oil appear on the surface.

6 SWIRL in the cream and sprinkle with the almonds. Serve hot with Naans (see page 26).

ROGAN JOSH *MUTTON MASALEDAAR*

SERVES 4   PREPARATION TIME: 20 MINUTES
COOKING TIME: 1 HOUR

From Kashmir in northern India, this is another restaurant favorite
that is very easy to cook at home.

3 tablespoons **vegetable oil**

1-inch piece **cinnamon stick**
  or **cassia bark**

3 **green cardamom pods**

2 **bay leaves**

2 **onions**, finely chopped

2 **garlic** cloves, finely chopped

1 tablespoon **butter** or **ghee**

¼ teaspoon **turmeric**

¼ teaspoon **chili powder**

½ teaspoon **ground cumin**

½ teaspoon **ground coriander**

1 teaspoon **tomato paste**

18 ounces boneless **stewing lamb**, chopped

¼ teaspoon **salt**

a pinch **Garam Masala** (*see page 23*)

1 teaspoon freshly squeezed **lemon juice**

1 **HEAT** the oil in a large flameproof casserole over medium heat. Add the cinnamon or cassia bark, the cardamom pods, and bay leaves and fry, stirring, 30 seconds, or until the spices splutter and you can smell their aroma. Watch them carefully so they do not burn.

2 **ADD** the onions, garlic, and butter or ghee and fry, stirring occasionally, 8 to 10 minutes until the onions caramelize.

3 **STIR** in the turmeric, chili powder, cumin, and coriander and stir about 30 seconds. Stir in the tomato paste.

4 **ADD** the lamb and fry 5 to 7 minutes until it looks brown.

5 **BRING** 1½ cups water to the boil while the lamb is frying. Pour the boiling water over the lamb. Return to the boil, then cover the pan, reduce the heat, and simmer 40 minutes, or until the meat is tender and droplets of oil appear on the surface.

6 **UNCOVER** the casserole, add the salt, and sprinkle over the garam masala, then stir in the lemon juice. Serve hot.

LUCKNOWI-STYLE LAMB BIRYANI

LUCKNOWI BIRYANI

SERVES **4** PREPARATION TIME: **10** MINUTES, PLUS COOKING THE RICE
COOKING TIME: **1** HOUR **30** MINUTES

Biryanis *are always prepared with basmati rice from India or Pakistan,
which retains its shape when cooked. A meal in itself, this dish takes
a little more time and practice than most, but it is worth the effort.*

6 tablespoons **butter** or **ghee**

heaped 1 cup **plain yogurt**, whisked

2-inch piece **gingerroot**, peeled and grated

½ teaspoon **salt**

¼ teaspoon **chili powder**

18 ounces boneless **stewing lamb**, chopped

15 to 20 **saffron strands**, soaked
in 2 tablespoons **milk**

1 teaspoon **Garam Masala** (*see page 23*)

1 recipe quantity **Plain Basmati Rice**
(*see page 31*), cooked

1 MELT 4 tablespoons of the butter or ghee in a large saucepan with
a tight-fitting lid over medium heat. Stir in the yogurt, ginger, salt, and
chili powder. Add the lamb and cook, stirring frequently, 5 minutes.

2 BRING 2 cups water to a boil while the lamb is cooking. Pour the
boiling water into the pan, cover, and simmer 45 to 50 minutes until
the meat is tender.

3 STIR the saffron-flavored milk and garam masala into the lamb.

4 SIMMER the lamb, uncovered, 5 to 7 minutes longer until most
of the water evaporates and you are left with a runny sauce.

5 PREHEAT the oven to 350°F and grease the bottom of a large
ovenproof casserole with 1 tablespoon of the butter or ghee.

6 PUT half of the meat in the casserole. Cover with half the cooked
rice, then layer with the remaining lamb and rice. Dot the remaining
1 tablespoon butter or ghee over the top.

7 COVER the casserole and bake 20 to 25 minutes until all the liquid
is absorbed and the ingredients are hot. Serve immediately.

GROUND LAMB WITH CUMIN AND GINGER *KEEMA MASALA*

SERVES 4 PREPARATION TIME: 10 MINUTES
COOKING TIME: 20 MINUTES

This recipe can also be used as a filling for meat samosas. Simply use the pastry dough recipe on page 30 and follow the assembly and frying instructions in the recipe for Vegetable Samosas on page 36.

3 tablespoons **peanut oil**

4 **garlic** cloves, chopped

2 **onions**, chopped

2 **green chilies**, chopped

1 teaspoon **ground cumin**

1 teaspoon **ground coriander**

¼ teaspoon **turmeric**

¼ teaspoon **salt**

2 teaspoons **tomato paste**

18 ounces **ground lamb**

2-inch piece **gingerroot**, peeled and grated

¼ teaspoon **Garam Masala** *(see page 23)*

a few **cilantro leaves**

1 HEAT the oil in a large saucepan or wok over medium heat. Add the garlic, onions, and chilies and fry, stirring frequently, 6 to 8 minutes until the onions turn golden brown.

2 STIR in the cumin, ground coriander, turmeric, salt, and tomato paste, then reduce the heat and continue frying 1 minute longer.

3 ADD the lamb, increase the heat, and continue frying, stirring, 8 to 10 minutes, using a wooden spoon to break up the meat, until it is no longer pink.

4 ADD the ginger and garam masala, stir well, then sprinkle with the cilantro leaves. Serve hot with Chapatis (see page 29) and Cucumber Relish (see page 22).

ROAST LAMB WITH WARMING SPICES

RAAN MASALEDAAR

SERVES **4**   PREPARATION TIME: **10** MINUTES, PLUS AT LEAST **1** HOUR MARINATING TIME   COOKING TIME: **2** HOURS

This dish of yogurt-marinated and roasted leg of lamb comes from the border of northern India and Pakistan. It is a common delicacy in Northwest Frontier cuisine, where mutton is often used instead of lamb.

---

1 **leg of lamb** on the bone weighing 3 pounds 5 ounces

2-inch piece **gingerroot**, peeled and grated

1 **onion**, finely chopped

¼ cup **plain yogurt**, whisked

¼ cup **vegetable oil**

1 teaspoon **Garam Masala** (*see page 23*)

½ teaspoon **chili powder**

½ teaspoon **salt**

1 PRICK the flesh of the lamb all over with a skewer or sharp knife.

2 PUT the ginger, onion, yogurt, oil, garam masala, chili powder, and salt in a large bowl and mix well.

3 ADD the lamb to the bowl and use your hands to smear the marinade all over the lamb, then cover and place in the refrigerator at least 1 hour, or overnight if time allows. Remove the lamb from the refrigerator 20 minutes before cooking.

4 PREHEAT the oven to 350°F.

5 PUT the lamb in a roasting pan, cover with foil, and roast 2 hours. Baste with the juices in the pan after 1 hour, then continue roasting the remaining 1 hour, or until the flesh is tender when you pierce it with a fork.

6 REMOVE the lamb from the oven and let rest, still covered with the foil, about 15 minutes before carving and serving.

SPICED LAMB CHOPS *KARAHI LAMB*

**SERVES 4   PREPARATION TIME: 15 MINUTES
COOKING TIME: 25 MINUTES**

Karahi is a style of cooking that comes from Kashmir in northern India, where the curries are cooked in a cast-iron pan with a rounded base and two handles, also called a karahi. *A wok or large skillet with a cover makes an ideal substitute for preparing this particular comforting recipe.*

---

3 tablespoons **vegetable oil**

4 **lamb loin chops** (about 5 ounces each)

4 **garlic** cloves, finely chopped

2 **green chilies**, finely chopped

1 **onion**, finely chopped

4 **green cardamom pods**

1 teaspoon **ground cumin**

1 teaspoon **ground coriander**

¼ teaspoon **turmeric**

¼ teaspoon **ground cinnamon**

¼ teaspoon **salt**

2 tablespoons **tomato paste**

¼ teaspoon **Garam Masala** (*see page 23*)

2-inch piece **gingerroot**, peeled and grated

1 **HEAT** the oil in a wok or large skillet with a tight-fitting lid over medium heat. Add the lamb chops, garlic, chilies, onion, and cardamom pods and fry, stirring, 12 minutes, or until the lamb changes color. Bring 1¼ cups water to a boil while the lamb is cooking.

2 **STIR** the cumin, coriander, turmeric, cinnamon, and salt into the lamb and continue frying 1 minute longer. Add the tomato paste, then pour in the boiling water.

3 **COVER** the pan, reduce the heat to low, and simmer 12 minutes, or until droplets of oil appear on the surface. Sprinkle with the garam masala and ginger and serve hot with Naans (see page 26).

LAMB WITH PEAS AND RICE

KEEMA MATTAR CHAWAL

SERVES **4** PREPARATION TIME: **15** MINUTES, PLUS COOKING THE RICE
COOKING TIME: **15** MINUTES

1 tablespoon **tomato paste**

¼ cup **vegetable oil**

½ teaspoon **ground cumin**

½ teaspoon **ground coriander**

¼ teaspoon **turmeric**

¼ teaspoon **chili powder**

¼ teaspoon **Garam Masala** (*see page 23*)

¼ teaspoon **salt**

2 **garlic** cloves, chopped

1 **onion**, chopped

14 ounces **ground lamb**

1 cup shelled **peas**, thawed if frozen

1-inch piece **gingerroot**, peeled and grated

1 recipe quantity **Plain Basmati Rice**
   (*see page 31*), cooked

a few **cilantro leaves**

4 tablespoons **plain yogurt**

1 MIX the tomato paste with 1 tablespoon of the oil, the cumin, ground coriander, turmeric, chili powder, garam masala, and salt in a small bowl to form a thick paste; set aside.

2 HEAT the remaining 3 tablespoons oil in a large saucepan or wok over medium heat. Add the garlic and onion and fry, stirring, 1 minute.

3 ADD the ground lamb, increase the heat, and continue frying 8 to 10 minutes, using a wooden spoon to break up the meat, until it is no longer pink.

4 ADD the spice paste to the lamb and cook, stirring, 1½ minutes. Stir in the peas and ginger, then add the cooked rice and continue cooking, stirring, until the rice is hot. Sprinkle with cilantro leaves and top with a dollop of yogurt. Serve hot with extra yogurt.

GOAN PORK MEATBALLS IN SPICY CURRY

BOLINHAS DE CARNE

MAKES 16   PREPARATION TIME: 15 MINUTES
COOKING TIME: 30 TO 35 MINUTES

2-inch piece **gingerroot**, peeled and chopped

4 **garlic** cloves

2 **green chilies**, roughly chopped

½ teaspoon freshly ground **black pepper**

2½ tablespoons freshly squeezed **lemon juice**

½ teaspoon **salt**

18 ounces **ground pork**

2 tablespoons **rice flour**

about 5 tablespoons **peanut oil**

3 **tomatoes**, coarsely chopped

1 **onion**, chopped

½ teaspoon **paprika**

½ teaspoon **ground cumin**

½ teaspoon **ground coriander**

¼ teaspoon **chili powder**

½ teaspoon **Garam Masala** (*see page 23*)

1 **PUT** the ginger, garlic, chilies, black pepper, 2 tablespoons of the lemon juice, and ¼ teaspoon of salt in a blender and blend until a thick paste forms. Transfer the paste to a large bowl, add the pork, and mix well. Wet your hands and shape the mixture into 16 meatballs of equal size.

2 **ROLL** the meatballs in the rice flour so they are coated all over.

3 **HEAT** 2 tablespoons of the oil in a large skillet over medium-high heat. Add the meatballs and fry 3 minutes, turning them in the oil until they are light brown. Do this in batches, adding extra oil, if necessary. Remove the meatballs, wipe out the pan, and set aside.

4 **PUT** the tomatoes in the blender and blend until smooth; set aside.

5 **HEAT** 3 tablespoons of the oil in the pan over medium heat. Add the onion and fry, stirring occasionally, 6 to 8 minutes until golden brown. Stir the paprika, cumin, coriander, chili powder, ½ tablespoon of the lemon juice, and the remaining ¼ teaspoon salt into the onions and fry 30 seconds, or until you can smell the aroma of the spices. Bring 1 cup water to a boil while the mixture cooks.

6 **ADD** the tomatoes to the pan and mix well. Add the meatballs and stir in the boiling water. Bring to a boil, then reduce the heat and simmer, uncovered, 8 to 10 minutes until the meatballs are cooked. Sprinkle the garam masala over and serve with Plain Basmati Rice (see page 31).

PORK VINDALOO *VINDALHO DE PORCO*

SERVES 4   PREPARATION TIME: 15 MINUTES, PLUS AT LEAST
2 HOURS MARINATING TIME   COOKING TIME: 45 MINUTES

*Goanese cuisine is influenced by the region's large Christian communities
that eat beef and pork, which are taboo in most other parts of the country.*

10 **black peppercorns**

6 **cloves**

4 **green cardamom pods**

1 teaspoon **cumin seeds**

1 teaspoon **brown mustard seeds**

2-inch piece **gingerroot**, peeled and chopped

6 **garlic** cloves

1 **onion**, roughly chopped

1 **dried red chili**, chopped

½ teaspoon **turmeric**

½ teaspoon **ground cinnamon**

¼ teaspoon **chili powder**

2 tablespoons **malt vinegar** or **distilled
white vinegar**

1 teaspoon **tomato paste**

18 ounces boneless **leg of pork**, cut into
bite-size pieces

1 HEAT a dry skillet over medium-low heat until you can feel the heat
rising. Add the peppercorns, cloves, cardamom pods, cumin, and
mustard seeds and roast, shaking the pan occasionally, until you can
smell the aroma of the spices. Watch carefully so they do not burn.
Immediately tip the spices onto a plate and let cool completely.

2 TRANSFER the spices to a blender along with the ginger, garlic,
onion, dried chili, turmeric, cinnamon, chili powder, vinegar, and
tomato paste and blend until a coarse, thick paste forms.

3 PLACE the pork in a large, nonmetallic bowl. Add the paste and use
your hands to rub it into the meat. Cover the bowl with plastic wrap
and refrigerate at least 2 hours or overnight. Remove from the
refrigerator about 15 minutes before cooking.

4 HEAT the oil in a large saucepan with a tight-fitting lid. Add the
pork and fry 10 minutes, or until all the pieces are light brown.
Bring 1¾ cups water to a boil while the pork is cooking.

5 POUR the water into the pan and return to a boil. Reduce the heat,
cover, and simmer 25 to 30 minutes until the pork is tender. Serve hot
with Plain Basmati Rice (see page 31) and Mango Chutney (see page 19).

GOAN FISH CURRY *AMBOTIK*

SERVES 4   PREPARATION TIME: 15 MINUTES
COOKING TIME: 15 TO 20 MINUTES

½ teaspoon **salt**

1 pound skinless **lemon sole** or **hoki** filets,
    cut into 2½-inch pieces

1 teaspoon **tamarind pulp**

¼ cup crumbled **creamed coconut**

2-inch piece **gingerroot**, peeled
    and chopped

5 **garlic** cloves

1 teaspoon **sugar**

1 **dried red chili**, roughly chopped

¼ teaspoon **chili powder**

¼ teaspoon **turmeric**

¼ teaspoon **ground cumin**

¼ teaspoon **ground coriander**

¼ teaspoon freshly ground **black pepper**

¼ teaspoon **ground cinnamon**

3 tablespoons **peanut oil**

1 **onion**, finely chopped

1 **tomato**, chopped

1 SPRINKLE the salt over the fish and set aside.

2 PUT the tamarind pulp in a small heatproof bowl, pour
enough boiling water to cover over, and let stand 10 minutes.
Use a wooden spoon to press the pulp and release the seeds and fibers,
then strain through a nylon strainer into a bowl, pressing with the back
of the spoon to extract as much juice as possible. Discard the pulp.

3 TRANSFER the tamarind juice to a blender. Add the creamed
coconut, ginger, garlic, sugar, dried chili, chili powder, turmeric,
cumin, coriander, black pepper, cinnamon, 1 tablespoon of the oil,
and 1 tablespoon water and blend until the mixture forms a thick,
coarse paste.

4 HEAT the remaining 2 tablespoons oil in a large saucepan or wok
over medium heat. Add the onion and fry, stirring constantly,
6 to 8 minutes until golden brown. Add the tomato and continue
frying, stirring, 2 to 3 minutes until it is soft. Bring 1¼ cups water
to a boil while the tomato is cooking.

5 ADD the tamarind paste and boiling water to the pan and return
to a boil. Reduce the heat and simmer, uncovered, 2 minutes,
then add the fish to the pan, taking care not to break up the pieces.
Simmer 5 to 6 minutes longer until the fish is cooked through
and the flesh flakes easily, then serve.

HALIBUT WITH GREEN CHILIES AND CILANTRO

POTHAL CURRY

**SERVES 4   PREPARATION TIME: 10 MINUTES
COOKING TIME: 15 MINUTES**

½ teaspoon **turmeric**

¼ teaspoon **salt**

a pinch **chili powder**

4 boneless **halibut** filets (about 3¼ ounces each), skinned

2 tablespoons **tamarind pulp**

a handful **cilantro leaves**

2-inch piece **gingerroot**, peeled and chopped

4 **garlic** cloves

2 **green chilies**, chopped

1 teaspoon **ground cumin**

2 tablespoons **peanut oil**

1 SPRINKLE the turmeric, salt, and chili powder over the halibut and set aside.

2 PUT the tamarind pulp in a small heatproof bowl, pour enough boiling water to cover over, and let stand 10 minutes. Use a wooden spoon to press the pulp and release the seeds and fibers, then strain through a nylon strainer into a bowl, pressing with the back of the spoon to extract as much juice as possible. Discard the pulp, stir ¼ cup water into the tamarind juice, and set aside.

3 SET a few cilantro leaves aside. Chop the remaining ones and put them in a blender with the ginger, garlic, chilies, cumin, and ½ cup water. Blend until the mixture forms a coarse, watery paste.

4 HEAT the oil in a large skillet over medium heat. Add the fish and fry 3 to 4 minutes, turning once, until lightly browned on both sides; remove from the pan and set aside.

5 ADD the cilantro paste to the oil remaining in the pan and simmer about 3 minutes, stirring occasionally, until droplets of oil appear on the surface. Return the fish to the pan and simmer 1 minute.

6 POUR the tamarind juice into the pan. Simmer 1 minute longer, then serve with the remaining cilantro leaves.

WHITE FISH IN TOMATO CURRY

TAMATAR MACHCHI

**SERVES 4   PREPARATION TIME: 10 MINUTES
COOKING TIME: 20 MINUTES**

*Using only a few basic spices brings out the subtle and delicate flavors
of the fish in this quick and zesty dish. The white fish can also be replaced
with an oily fish, such as tuna or mackerel.*

½ teaspoon **turmeric**

¼ teaspoon **salt**

18 ounces skinless, boneless **sole**, **coley**, or **cod**
filets, cut into 3-inch pieces

3 tablespoons **vegetable oil**

2-inch piece **gingerroot**, peeled and chopped

5 **garlic** cloves, chopped

2 **onions**, finely chopped

2 large **plum tomatoes**, finely chopped

½ teaspoon **ground cumin**

½ teaspoon **ground coriander**

¼ teaspoon **chili powder**

1 SPRINKLE the turmeric and salt over the fish and set aside.

2 HEAT the oil in a large saucepan over medium heat. Add the ginger,
garlic, and onions and fry, stirring frequently, 6 to 8 minutes until the
onions are golden brown.

3 ADD the tomatoes, cumin, coriander, and chili powder and cook,
stirring, 2 minutes. Bring ¾ cup water to a boil.

4 PUT the fish in the pan and simmer 2 minutes longer, taking care not
to break up the pieces.

5 POUR the boiling water over and simmer 8 to 9 minutes longer until
the fish is cooked through and the flesh flakes easily. Serve hot with
Potatoes with Cauliflower (see page 72) and Chapatis (see page 29).

SPICED WHITE FISH COOKED IN COCONUT

MEEN MOLEE

SERVES 4   PREPARATION TIME: 10 MINUTES
COOKING TIME: 15 MINUTES

The combination of the coconut and tamarind gives this dish a distinctive sweet-and-sour flavor that is typical of Kerala, in the south of India.

2 tablespoons **tamarind pulp**

1 teaspoon **ground cumin**

1 teaspoon **ground coriander**

a pinch **chili powder**

¼ teaspoon **turmeric**

¼ teaspoon **salt**

10 ounces **lemon sole** filets, skinned, trimmed, and cut into 3-inch pieces

2 tablespoons **vegetable oil**

4 **garlic** cloves, chopped

3½ tablespoons crumbled **creamed coconut**

1 **PUT** the tamarind pulp in a small heatproof bowl, pour enough boiling water to cover over, and let stand 10 minutes. Use a wooden spoon to press the pulp and release the seeds and fibers, then strain through a nylon strainer into a bowl, pressing with the back of the spoon to extract as much juice as possible. Discard the pulp. Bring 1 cup water to a boil.

2 **SPRINKLE** the turmeric and salt over the fish. Stir the cumin, coriander, chili powder, and boiling water into the tamarind juice, then set aside.

3 **HEAT** the oil in a large skillet over medium heat. Add the fish and fry 3 to 4 minutes, turning occasionally and taking care not to break up the pieces. Remove the fish from the pan and set aside.

4 **REDUCE** the heat. Add the garlic to the oil remaining in the pan, and fry, stirring, 30 seconds, or until golden. Watch so it does not burn.

5 **RETURN** the fish to the pan. Stir in the creamed coconut, tamarind liquid, and ¼ cup boiling water. Simmer 3 to 4 minutes longer until the flavors blend and the fish is cooked through and flakes easily. Serve hot with Plain Basmati Rice (see page 31).

TANDOORI-STYLE TROUT

TANDOORI MACHCHI

**SERVES 4   PREPARATION TIME: 10 MINUTES, PLUS 30 MINUTES
MARINATING TIME   COOKING TIME: 15 MINUTES**

*Like all tandoori dishes, this tender, flaky trout dish can also be cooked on
a barbecue—turning an outdoor summer meal into a truly special occasion.*

---

4 whole **trout**, cleaned

2-inch piece **gingerroot**, peeled
  and coarsely chopped

6 **garlic** cloves

3 tablespoons **vegetable oil**

1 tablespoon freshly squeezed **lemon juice**

2 teaspoons **tomato paste**

1 teaspoon **paprika**

½ teaspoon **chili powder**

½ teaspoon **ground cumin**

½ teaspoon **salt**

¼ teaspoon **turmeric**

a few **cilantro leaves**

1 **CUT** 4 diagonal slits in each trout, 2 on each side. Place the fish on
a deep, nonmetallic dish large enough to hold them in a single layer.

2 **PUT** all the remaining ingredients, except the cilantro leaves, in
a blender and blend until a coarse paste forms.

3 **POUR** the paste over the trout and rub it into the flesh and the
slits. Cover the dish with plastic wrap and place it in the refrigerator
30 minutes to let the marinade soak into the fish.

4 **PREHEAT** the broiler to medium. Place the fish on a foil-lined broiler
pan and broil 7 to 8 minutes on each side until the skin blisters and
the fish is white and flaky inside when you cut along the backbone.
Serve with the cilantro leaves, Cilantro Chutney (see page 19), and
Tomato, Onion, and Chili Salad (see page 160).

TUNA WITH PICKLING SPICES

MAACHER JHOL

**SERVES 4   PREPARATION TIME: 10 MINUTES
COOKING TIME: 25 TO 30 MINUTES**

The aromatic spice blend panch phoron features many of the spices used to make Indian pickles. Here, it lends a distinct pungent flavor to seared tuna steaks.

1 teaspoon **salt**

1 teaspoon **turmeric**

4 **tuna steaks**

5 tablespoons **peanut oil**

1 teaspoon **Panch Phoron** (*see page 24*)

2 **potatoes**, peeled and quartered

2-inch piece **gingerroot**, peeled

6 **garlic** cloves

4 **green chilies**

a pinch **chili powder**

a few **cilantro leaves**

1 SPRINKLE the salt and turmeric over the tuna. Heat 4 tablespoons of the oil in a large skillet over medium heat, then add the tuna steaks and lightly fry on each side 3 minutes, or until they are seared. Remove them from the pan and set aside.

2 ADD the remaining 1 tablespoon oil to the pan. Tip in the panch phoron and fry about 30 seconds, stirring constantly, or until you can smell the aroma. Watch carefully so the mixture does not burn.

3 ADD the potatoes and fry about 5 minutes, stirring occasionally. Bring 2 cups water to a boil.

4 PUT the ginger, garlic, chilies, and chili powder in a blender and blend until a coarse paste forms. Tip the paste into the pan and continue frying 2 minutes longer.

5 STIR in the boiling water and return to a boil. Reduce the heat and simmer 6 to 7 minutes longer until the potatoes are tender.

6 RETURN the tuna to the pan and simmer 4 minutes longer, or until the fish is cooked to your liking. Serve hot, sprinkled with the cilantro leaves.

MALABAR SHRIMP CURRY

CHEMMEEN CURRY

SERVES 4   PREPARATION TIME: 10 MINUTES
COOKING TIME: 15 TO 20 MINUTES

Velvety coconut milk and succulent seafood, the signature elements of Malabar cuisine, combine here in a mouthwatering curry.

½ teaspoon **turmeric**

½ teaspoon **salt**

20 raw **jumbo shrimp**, shelled and black veins removed (*see page 18*)

¼ cup **peanut oil**

2-inch piece **gingerroot**, peeled and grated

8 **shallots**, chopped

6 **garlic** cloves, chopped

2 **green chilies**, chopped

2 **tomatoes**, chopped

a pinch **chili powder** (optional)

1¼ cups **coconut milk**

8 **curry leaves**

½ teaspoon **brown mustard seeds**

1 **SPRINKLE** the turmeric and salt over the shrimp and set aside.

2 **HEAT** 3 tablespoons of the oil in a large skillet over medium heat. Add the ginger, shallots, garlic, and green chilies and fry, stirring occasionally, 6 to 8 minutes until the shallots are golden brown. Bring ½ cup water to a boil.

3 **ADD** the tomatoes and chili powder, if using, and fry 2 minutes longer, then add the shrimp and continue stirring 2 minutes.

4 **POUR** the coconut milk into the pan with the boiling water and simmer 2 minutes, or just until the shrimp turn opaque.

5 **HEAT** the remaining 1 tablespoon oil in a small skillet over medium heat. Add the curry leaves and mustard seeds and fry 30 seconds, or until the seeds splutter. Watch carefully so the leaves and seeds do not burn. Stir them into the shrimp curry. Serve hot.

SHRIMP WITH GARLIC AND CHILI

JHINGA PATIA

SERVES 4 PREPARATION TIME: 20 MINUTES
COOKING TIME: 12 MINUTES

Piquant tomato paste adds a level of flavor to these spicy and succulent shrimp.

¼ cup **peanut oil**

1 **onion**, chopped

6 **garlic** cloves, crushed

½ teaspoon **ground cumin**

½ teaspoon **salt**

¼ teaspoon **turmeric**

¼ teaspoon **ground coriander**

¼ teaspoon **chili powder**

1 tablespoon **tomato paste**

14 ounces **jumbo shrimp**, shelled and black veins removed (*see page 18*)

¼ teaspoon **Garam Masala** (*see page 23*)

a few **cilantro leaves**, chopped

1 HEAT the oil in a large skillet over medium heat. Add the onion and fry, stirring frequently, 6 to 8 minutes until golden brown. Bring ½ cup water to a boil, while the onions fry.

2 ADD the garlic, cumin, salt, turmeric, ground coriander, chili powder, and tomato paste to the onion and continue frying, stirring constantly, 1 minute. Tip in the shrimp and fry, stirring, 2 to 3 minutes.

3 POUR the boiling water over and fry 1 minute longer, or just until the shrimp turn opaque and curl.

4 SPRINKLE the garam masala and cilantro leaves over the dish. Serve hot with Spiced Rice (see page 32).

SHRIMP WITH HOT-AND-SOUR CURRY

KOLAMBICHE KAALVAN

SERVES 4   PREPARATION TIME: 10 MINUTES
COOKING TIME: 5 TO 6 MINUTES

A kaalvan *is a thin gravy-based dish made with meat, poultry, or seafood. A traditional recipe from the western state of Maharashtra, it can also be made with fish, such as pomfret or cod.*

---

2 tablespoons **tamarind pulp**

1 teaspoon **ground cumin**

1 teaspoon **ground coriander**

1 teaspoon **rice flour**

½ teaspoon **chili powder**

½ teaspoon **turmeric**

¼ teaspoon **salt**

14 ounces raw **jumbo shrimp**, shelled and black veins removed (*see page 18*)

2 tablespoons **peanut oil**

4 **garlic** cloves, slightly crushed

a few **cilantro leaves**

1 **PUT** the tamarind pulp in a small heatproof bowl, pour enough boiling water to cover over, and let stand 10 minutes. Use a wooden spoon to press the pulp and release the seeds and fibers, then strain through a nylon strainer into a bowl, pressing with the back of the spoon to extract as much juice as possible. Discard the pulp.

2 **ADD** the cumin, ground coriander, rice flour, chili powder, and turmeric to the tamarind juice and stir to make a lumpy paste.

3 **BRING** 1¾ cups water to a boil. Sprinkle the salt over the shrimp. Heat the oil in a large wok or skillet over medium heat. Add the shrimp and garlic and fry, stirring constantly, 1 minute. Stir in the tamarind paste and continue frying, stirring, 1 minute longer.

4 **POUR** the boiling water over and simmer 3 minutes longer, stirring occasionally, or just until the shrimp turn opaque and curl. Scatter with cilantro leaves and serve.

BALTI POTATOES *HARYALI ALOO*

**SERVES 4 PREPARATION TIME: 15 MINUTES
COOKING TIME: 30 TO 35 MINUTES**

Balti *means bucket and is the name given to a style of cuisine that in all probability was developed in Birmingham, England. Balti-style dishes are named after the pot or vessel in which they are cooked and served, although a wok works just as well for cooking in. This dish is a lovely accompaniment to lamb.*

2¼ pounds **waxy potatoes**, peeled and cut into 2-inch pieces

¼ cup **vegetable oil**

2 **onions**, finely chopped

1 bunch **cilantro leaves**

a few **mint leaves**

2-inch piece **gingerroot**, peeled and coarsely chopped

4 **garlic** cloves

3 **green chilies**, chopped

½ teaspoon **salt**

¼ teaspoon **turmeric**

1 BRING a large saucepan of water to a boil over high heat. Add the potatoes, return the water to a boil, and continue boiling 10 minutes, or until the potatoes are almost tender; drain and set aside.

2 HEAT the oil in a wok over medium heat. Add the onions and fry, stirring frequently, 6 to 8 minutes until they are golden brown.

3 PUT the cilantro, mint, ginger, garlic, and chilies in a blender and blend until the mixture forms a coarse paste. Bring 1¾ cups water to a boil.

4 STIR the salt and turmeric into the onions and cook 1 minute, then add the cilantro paste and continue frying, stirring constantly, 3 to 4 minutes. Add the potatoes and fry, stirring, 3 minutes longer.

5 POUR the boiling water over and return to a boil. Reduce the heat and simmer, uncovered, 6 to 7 minutes until the potatoes are tender, then serve.

MAHARASHTRIAN LENTILS *VARAN*

SERVES 4   PREPARATION TIME: 5 MINUTES
COOKING TIME: 30 MINUTES

The cuisine of Maharashtra, in western India, varies from extremely mild in flavor to alarmingly hot. This simple yet flavorsome dal, *or lentil stew, seasoned only with turmeric and asafoetida, is a comforting dish that perfectly complements fiery hot curries.*

1¼ cups **split yellow lentils**

½ teaspoon **turmeric**

¼ cup **butter** or **ghee**

1 teaspoon **sugar**

½ teaspoon **salt**

a pinch **asafoetida**

a few **cilantro leaves**

1 PUT 2½ cups water in a large saucepan and bring to a boil over high heat. Add the lentils and turmeric to the pan and return to a boil. Partially cover the pan, reduce the heat to low, and simmer, stirring occasionally, 25 minutes, or until the lentils are mushy. Watch carefully so the lentils do not burn. Top up with extra boiling water, if necessary.

2 MELT the butter or ghee in another pan over medium heat, then stir in the sugar, salt, and asafoetida. Add this mixture to the lentils. Bring 1¼ cups water to a boil and stir into the lentils.

3 MASH the lentils a little against the side of the pan and simmer 3 minutes longer. Serve hot, garnished with the cilantro leaves.

TEMPERED RED LENTILS

TARKA DAL

**SERVES 4   PREPARATION TIME: 10 MINUTES
COOKING TIME: 30 MINUTES**

*Lentils are prepared almost daily in many Indian homes. This recipe
produces a rich velvety puree laced with spiced butter, simply made
by boiling the lentils, then mashing them and pouring spicy butter
over the top. This technique is called tempering.*

heaped 1 cup **split red lentils**

3 tablespoons **butter** or **ghee**

6 **curry leaves**

1 **green chili**, chopped

½ teaspoon **brown mustard seeds**

½ teaspoon **turmeric**

¼ teaspoon **salt**

a pinch **asafoetida**

1 BRING 2 cups water to a boil in a large saucepan over high heat.
Add the lentils and return the water to a boil. Partially cover the pan,
reduce the heat to low, and simmer, uncovered, stirring occasionally,
20 to 30 minutes until the mixture becomes mushy. Watch carefully
so the lentils do not burn. Top up with extra boiling water, if necessary.

2 MELT the butter in a skillet over medium heat. Add the curry leaves,
chili, mustard seeds, turmeric, salt, and asafoetida and fry, stirring
constantly, 30 seconds, or until the spices splutter. Watch carefully
so they do not burn.

3 STIR the buttery spice mixture into the lentils, then cook 2 minutes
longer. Serve hot with Okra with Mustard Seeds (see page 158).

SPICED BLACK-EYED PEAS

RAUNGI

**SERVES 4   PREPARATION TIME: 10 MINUTES
COOKING TIME: 12 MINUTES**

Black-eyed peas, often eaten after prayers in southern India, have a fine, almost nutty flavor. The addition of yogurt, ginger, and cumin in this recipe results in a comforting and flavorsome dish that can be enjoyed with any favorite meat or vegetarian main dish.

3 tablespoons **vegetable oil**

2 cans (14 ounces each) **black-eyed peas**, drained and rinsed

½ teaspoon **turmeric**

a pinch **asafoetida**

1 teaspoon **ground cumin**

½ teaspoon **salt**

¼ teaspoon **chili powder**

¼ cup **plain yogurt**, whisked

2-inch piece **gingerroot**, peeled and grated

a few **cilantro leaves**, chopped

1 HEAT the oil in a large saucepan over medium heat. Add the beans, turmeric, and asafoetida and stir 1 minute, or until you can smell the aroma of the spices.

2 STIR the cumin, salt, and chili powder. Bring ¾ cup water to a boil.

3 POUR the boiling water over, add the yogurt, and stir well. Cover the pan, reduce the heat, and simmer 6 to 8 minutes until droplets of oil appear on the surface.

4 SPRINKLE with the ginger and cilantro leaves, then serve hot with Chapatis (see page 29) and Cucumber Relish (see page 22).

SMOKED EGGPLANT

BAINGAN BHARTA

**SERVES 4   PREPARATION TIME: 15 TO 20 MINUTES
COOKING TIME: 15 MINUTES**

This earthy, aromatic vegetable dish from North India is a wonderful accompaniment to any main meal.

2 large **eggplants**

3 tablespoons **vegetable oil**, plus extra for charring the eggplants (optional)

6 **garlic** cloves, finely chopped

2 **onions**, finely chopped

2 **green chilies**, finely chopped

2 teaspoons **tomato paste**

1 teaspoon **ground cumin**

¼ teaspoon **salt**

1-inch piece **gingerroot**, peeled and grated

a pinch **Garam Masala** (*see page 23*)

a few **cilantro leaves**, chopped

1 HOLD an eggplant with a pair of tongs over a flame, turning often, until the skin chars and blisters all over. Repeat with the other eggplant. Alternatively, preheat the broiler to high, halve each eggplant, and rub the cut surface with a little oil. Place the eggplants, cut sides down, on a broiler pan and broil 8 to 10 minutes until the skin chars and blisters.

2 LEAVE the eggplants until they are cool enough to handle. Cut each one in half lengthwise, if they are still whole, and scoop the flesh into a bowl, then mash or chop it and set aside.

3 HEAT the oil in a wok or large saucepan over medium heat. Add the garlic, onions, and chilies and fry, stirring frequently, 6 to 8 minutes until the onions are golden brown.

4 ADD the tomato paste, cumin, and salt and fry, stirring, 2 minutes until the mixture becomes very thick. Stir in the eggplant and cook, stirring, 3 minutes until the mixture becomes thick and mushy.

5 SPRINKLE with the ginger and garam masala and continue cooking 30 seconds. Serve hot, sprinkled with cilantro leaves.

CUMIN-INFUSED PEAS

ZEERAWALI MATTAR

SERVES 4   PREPARATION TIME: 2 MINUTES
COOKING TIME: 5 MINUTES

This quick recipe uses a few basic spices to jazz up fresh peas—and is versatile enough to be served hot, chilled, or at room temperature. If you cannot get hold of fresh peas, frozen ones provide a good alternative once thawed.

---

2 tablespoons **vegetable oil**

½ teaspoon **brown mustard seeds**

1 teaspoon **ground cumin**

½ teaspoon **ground coriander**

¼ teaspoon **chili powder**

¼ teaspoon **turmeric**

¼ teaspoon **salt**

2 cups shelled **peas**, thawed if frozen

1 teaspoon freshly squeezed **lemon juice**

1 HEAT the oil in a large skillet over medium heat. Add the mustard seeds and fry, stirring constantly, 30 seconds, or until they splutter. Watch carefully so they do not burn.

2 STIR in the cumin, coriander, chili powder, turmeric, salt, and peas and continue frying 2 minutes longer.

3 SPRINKLE the lemon juice and 2 tablespoons water over the peas. Continue cooking 1 minute longer, or until the peas are tender. Serve hot, or cool completely, cover, and refrigerate until required.

GREEN BEANS WITH GARLIC AND MUSTARD SEEDS

LAHSUNI RAI BEANS

SERVES 4   PREPARATION TIME: 10 MINUTES
COOKING TIME: 8 MINUTES

Mustard seeds are to southern, southwestern, and eastern India what cumin seeds are to the north. Used to season just about every savory preparation, they evoke a hot and nutty flavor once they are heated in oil.

3 tablespoons **peanut oil**

½ teaspoon **brown mustard seeds**

3 **garlic** cloves, chopped

2 **green chilies**, finely chopped

1 **onion**, finely chopped

14 ounces fine **green beans**, topped and tailed

1 teaspoon **ground cumin**

¼ teaspoon **salt**

1 **HEAT** the oil in a large skillet over medium heat. Add the mustard seeds and fry, stirring constantly, 30 seconds, or until they splutter. Watch carefully so they do not burn.

2 **ADD** the garlic, chilies, and onion and continue frying, stirring frequently, 3 minutes, or until the onions become soft. Add the beans and fry 1 minute longer.

3 **STIR** in the cumin and salt and continue frying 2 to 3 minutes, or until the beans are tender. Serve hot.

GREEN PEPPERS WITH CUMIN

SHIMLA MIRCH SABZI

**SERVES 4   PREPARATION TIME: 5 MINUTES
COOKING TIME: 10 MINUTES**

*A touch of turmeric and tomato paste adds a warm golden glow to a quick
and colorful dish that is prepared in a matter of minutes.*

2 tablespoons **vegetable oil**

2 **garlic** cloves, sliced

1 **onion**, sliced

4 **green bell peppers**, seeded and cut
   into strips 1-inch thick

1 **green chili**, chopped

¼ teaspoon **turmeric**

1 teaspoon **ground cumin**

¼ teaspoon **salt**

1 **tomato**, chopped

1 teaspoon **tomato paste**

a pinch **Garam Masala** (*see page 23*)

1 HEAT the oil in a large saucepan over medium heat. Add the garlic
and onion and fry, stirring frequently, 2 minutes, or until the onion
starts to soften.

2 ADD the peppers, chili, turmeric, cumin, and salt and continue
frying 2 minutes. Stir in the chopped tomato and continue frying
2 minutes longer until the tomato starts to soften.

3 STIR in the tomato paste and continue cooking, stirring, 2 minutes,
or until the peppers are tender.

4 STIR in the garam masala and serve hot with Fried Legumes (see page
64) and Chapatis (see page 29).

CABBAGE WITH RED CHILIES

PATTA GOBHI KI SABZI

**SERVES 4 PREPARATION TIME: 5 MINUTES
COOKING TIME: 7 MINUTES**

Indian cooks from the south use coconut as frequently as cooks in the north use onions—and it features in both sweet and savory dishes. The shredded coconut in this recipe can be replaced with freshly grated coconut.

3 tablespoons **vegetable oil**

2 **dried red chilies**

1 teaspoon **brown mustard seeds**

4¼ cups finely shredded **white cabbage**

½ teaspoon **salt**

1 teaspoon freshly squeezed **lemon juice**

1 tablespoon **shredded coconut**

1 HEAT the oil in a large skillet or wok over medium heat. Add the chilies and mustard seeds and fry 30 seconds, stirring constantly, or until they begin to splutter. Watch carefully so they do not burn.

2 ADD the cabbage and salt, then increase the heat to medium-high. Fry, stirring constantly, 5 to 6 minutes until the cabbage is tender.

3 STIR in the lemon juice and coconut. Serve hot.

SPICED GREENS

HARI SABZI

SERVES 4   PREPARATION TIME: 5 MINUTES
COOKING TIME: 11 MINUTES

Indians use a wide variety of leafy greens in their cooking, including radish, carrot, pumpkin, and turnip leaves. Kale makes a good substitute for the greens in this dish, which is traditionally prepared with potatoes, beans, or peas.

2 tablespoons **vegetable oil**

2 **garlic** cloves, crushed

1 **green chili**, chopped

½ teaspoon **salt**

1 pound chopped **leafy greens**, such as **savoy cabbage**

1 HEAT the oil in a large skillet or wok over medium-high heat. Add the garlic and fry, stirring, 30 seconds. Watch carefully to make sure the garlic does not burn.

2 ADD the chili, salt, and greens and fry, stirring constantly, 10 minutes, or until the greens are tender. Serve hot with Tempered Red Lentils (see page 142).

OKRA WITH MUSTARD SEEDS

RAI BHINDI

**SERVES 4   PREPARATION TIME: 15 MINUTES
COOKING TIME: 12 MINUTES**

Okra, also known as ladies' fingers because of its long, slender shape, is a favorite of many Indian cooks. In this dry dish, the lightly spiced okra remains deliciously crisp, and the mustard and cumin impart a subtle nutty flavor. It is essential to dry the okra thoroughly after rinsing to prevent the dish from becoming soggy when cooked.

1 pound **okra**, well rinsed and thoroughly dried

3 tablespoons **vegetable oil**

½ teaspoon **brown mustard seeds**

1 **green chili**, finely chopped

½ teaspoon **ground cumin**

¼ teaspoon **salt**

1 TRIM the stems off the okra and cut the pods into 1-inch long pieces.

2 HEAT the oil in a large skillet or wok over medium heat. Add the mustard seeds and fry, stirring, 30 to 40 seconds, or until they splutter. Watch carefully so they do not burn.

3 STIR in the remaining ingredients and increase the heat to medium-high. Continue frying, stirring constantly, 10 to 12 minutes until the okra is tender, then serve.

TOMATO, ONION, AND CHILI SALAD

TAMATAR PYAAZ AUR MIRCH KA SALAAD

SERVES 4   PREPARATION TIME: 10 MINUTES, PLUS CHILLING

Indian salads are refreshing complements to elaborate dishes that are loaded with spices and flavors. This sharp, tangy recipe is remarkably simple and pairs well with meat or chicken.

2 **tomatoes**, chopped

1 **red onion**, finely chopped

1 **green chili**, finely chopped

1 tablespoon freshly squeezed **lemon juice**

½ teaspoon **sugar**

a pinch freshly ground **black pepper**

a pinch **salt**

1 PUT all the ingredients in a nonmetallic bowl and toss together.

2 COVER the bowl with plastic wrap and refrigerate until required. Taste and adjust the seasoning, adding more salt and pepper, if necessary, just before serving. Serve chilled.

CARROT SALAD

KOSHIMBIR

SERVES 4   PREPARATION TIME: 10 MINUTES, PLUS CHILLING
COOKING TIME: 3 MINUTES

This Maharashtrian salad, from western India, can also be made with various other vegetables, such as radish or cabbage. More often than not, crushed or ground peanuts are added, as in this recipe, which is a perfect complement to any mild curry.

4 **carrots,** peeled and coarsely grated

1 **onion,** finely chopped

1 **green chili,** finely chopped

1 **tomato,** finely chopped

2 tablespoons freshly squeezed **lemon juice**

1 teaspoon **sugar**

½ teaspoon **salt**

2 tablespoons **roasted peanuts,** crushed (optional)

1 tablespoon **peanut oil**

6 **curry leaves**

½ teaspoon **brown** or **black mustard seeds**

¼ teaspoon **turmeric**

1 PUT the carrots, onion, chili, tomato, lemon juice, sugar, salt, and peanuts, if using, in a large bowl and mix well; set aside.

2 HEAT the oil in a skillet over medium-high heat. Add the curry leaves and mustard seeds and fry, stirring constantly, 30 seconds, or until they splutter. Watch carefully so the mixture does not burn.

3 ADD the turmeric, then drizzle the hot mixture over the salad, and stir well.

4 SET ASIDE until the salad cools completely, then cover the bowl with plastic wrap and refrigerate until required. Serve chilled.

SPROUTED MUNG BEAN SALAD

MOONG SALAAD

SERVES 4   PREPARATION TIME: 10 MINUTES, PLUS CHILLING
COOKING TIME: 2 MINUTES

Sprouted beans are easy to digest and are frequently used in dishes from the western and southern parts of India. They impart a crisp, nutty flavor to dishes like this one.

3 cups fresh **mung bean sprouts** (*see page 18*)

a pinch **turmeric**

1 **green chili**, finely chopped

1 **onion**, finely chopped

2 tablespoons freshly squeezed **lemon juice**

½ teaspoon **sugar**

½ teaspoon **salt**

a large pinch freshly ground **black pepper**

1 PUT the sprouts, turmeric, and 2 tablespoons water into a saucepan. Cook over medium heat, stirring, 2 minutes, or until the sprouts wilt.

2 MIX the chili, onion, lemon juice, sugar, salt, and pepper together in a large bowl.

3 ADD the cooked sprouts to the chili mixture and set aside to cool completely. Cover the bowl with plastic wrap and refrigerate until required. Serve chilled.

CHICKPEA PETIT FOURS

BESAN KI LADDOO

MAKES 16   PREPARATION TIME: 5 MINUTES, PLUS COOLING AND SETTING COOKING TIME: 11 MINUTES

These small, nutty-tasting treats are served aa an afternoon snack or often at the end of a meal in Indian homes. For an even richer taste, add five or six coarsely chopped almonds with their skins to the mixture after adding the sugar.

½ cup **unsalted butter**

1½ cups plus 2 tablespoons **chickpea or gram flour**, sifted

2 tablespoons **milk**

½ cup **sugar**

1 **PUT** the butter and chickpea or gram flour in a saucepan over medium heat and stir about 10 minutes, or until the butter melts, the flour looks like wet sand, and you can smell the nutty roasted aroma. Watch carefully so the mixture does not burn.

2 **STIR** in the milk, then remove the pan from the heat.

3 **ADD** the sugar and mix thoroughly with a fork 2 to 3 minutes until the mixture becomes thick and clumpy. Transfer it to a plate and set aside about 5 minutes, or until it is cool enough to handle.

4 **WET** your hands and shape the mixture into 16 balls of equal size.

5 **LEAVE** the balls to cool completely. Serve at room temperature, with Spicy Tea (see page 186). These petit fours can be stored in an airtight container at room temperature up to 10 days, or refrigerated up to 2 weeks.

CASHEW NUT DIAMONDS

KAAJU KI BARFI

MAKES **12** TO **14** DIAMONDS   PREPARATION TIME: **10** MINUTES, PLUS
A LITTLE COOLING TIME   COOKING TIME: **4** MINUTES

This fragrant, fudgelike Indian dessert is served during auspicious Hindu festivals.

1½ cups **cashew nuts**

seeds from 2 **green cardamom pods**
   (see page 14)

scant ½ cup **powdered sugar**

1 PUT the cashew nuts in a heatproof bowl and pour enough boiling
water to cover over, then set aside and let soak 10 minutes.

2 CRUSH the cardamom seeds to a powder in a mortar and pestle.

3 DRAIN the cashew nuts, put them in a blender, and blend until
the mixture forms a thick paste; set aside.

4 PUT the sugar in a saucepan over medium heat and cook, stirring
constantly, 2 minutes, or until the sugar melts.

5 STIR in the cashew nut paste and ground cardamom seeds. Spoon the
mixture onto waxed paper and use a wet metal spatula to spread it into
a 4-inch square, about ½ inch thick. Using a sharp knife, cut the square
into diamonds and let cool. Serve at room temperature, or transfer
to an airtight container and refrigerate up to 2 weeks.

COCONUT TREATS

NARIYAL LADDOO

MAKES 10 TO 12   PREPARATION TIME: 10 MINUTES
COOKING TIME: 4 MINUTES

Made with only two ingredients, this simple recipe is bursting with delicious sweetness. You can use store-bought coconut powder, but making your own from shredded coconut is easy and adds a distinct freshness to the finished dessert.

heaped 1 cup **shredded coconut**

scant ½ cup **sweetened condensed milk**

1 PUT the shredded coconut in a spice mill and grind to a fine powder.

2 POUR the condensed milk into a small saucepan and warm over low heat. Add all but 1½ tablespoons of the coconut powder and simmer 2 to 3 minutes, stirring constantly, until the mixture leaves the side of the pan. Watch carefully so it does not burn.

3 REMOVE the pan from the heat and set aside until the coconut mixture is just cool enough to handle.

4 SPRINKLE the remaining coconut powder onto a plate. Wet your hands and shape the mixture into 10 to 12 balls of equal size. Roll each ball in the coconut powder to cover evenly. Serve immediately, or transfer to an airtight container and refrigerate 5 to 6 days.

EXOTIC FRUIT SALAD

PHALON KA SALAAD

SERVES 4   PREPARATION TIME: 10 MINUTES, PLUS CHILLING TIME

Mango, the national fruit of India, is also known traditionally as the food of the gods. Its leaves are used as floral decorations during Hindu marriages and religious ceremonies. Used in all sorts of sweet preparations, mangoes are delicious eaten on their own or with other fruits, such as in this refreshing salad.

1 **papaya**

1 **mango**

1 **banana**, sliced

1 handful **strawberries**, hulled

2 teaspoons freshly squeezed **lime juice**

2 teaspoons **demerara** or **dark brown sugar**

1 PEEL the papaya with a knife, then cut it lengthwise, scoop out and discard the seeds, and cut the flesh into 1-inch pieces.

2 SLICE the mango lengthwise along each side of the large, flat seed. Place the 2 sides flesh side up and make criss-cross cuts into the flesh without cutting through the skin. Push the skin gently to make the cubes stand out, then cut away the segments of flesh.

3 COMBINE the papaya and mango with the remaining ingredients in a large bowl, cover with plastic wrap, and refrigerate. Remove from the refrigerator about 30 minutes before serving to let the salad return to room temperature. Mix well before serving. This can be refrigerated, covered, up to 2 days.

CARDAMOM ICE CREAM

ELAICHI KULFI

SERVES **4**   PREPARATION TIME: **10** MINUTES, PLUS AT LEAST **6** HOURS
FREEZING TIME   COOKING TIME: **5** MINUTES

*Traditionally made with boiled buffalo's milk, ice cream was brought
to Pakistan and India by the Moghuls from Persia in the 1500s. It later
found its way to the West as the result of colonization and immigration.
This rich, velvety version makes a satisfying end to any meal.*

½ teaspoon **cornstarch**

2 tablespoons **milk**

1 cup plus 2 tablespoons **evaporated milk**

1 cup plus 2 tablespoons **sweetened
    condensed milk**

¾ cup plus 2 tablespoons **heavy cream**

seeds from 3 **green cardamom pods**,
    crushed (*see page 14*)

1 PUT the cornstarch in a small bowl and slowly stir in the milk until
blended, then set aside.

2 POUR the evaporated milk into a saucepan and bring to a boil over
high heat. Add the condensed milk, heavy cream, cardamom seeds,
and the cornstarch mixture to the evaporated milk and continue
boiling, stirring constantly, 1 minute longer.

3 REMOVE the pan from the heat and let the ice cream mixture
cool slightly.

4 TRANSFER the mixture to a blender or food processor, or use
a hand-held mixer, and blend 2 minutes, or until smooth.

5 POUR the mixture into a freezerproof container with a lid and freeze
at least 6 hours, or ideally overnight, until the ice cream is set. Take the
ice cream out of the freezer 10 to 15 minutes before serving to let it
soften slightly. Serve 2 small scoops per person.

RICE PUDDING *KHEER*

SERVES 4   PREPARATION TIME: 10 MINUTES
COOKING TIME: 20 MINUTES

Rice plays an integral role in Indian culture and lifestyle and is served at many Hindu festivals. On New Year's Day, sweet rice pudding is served to mark a new beginning. This creamy cardamom-spiced rice pudding is delectable hot or cold.

5 **pistachio nuts**, shelled

5 **almonds**, shelled

2½ cups **whole milk**

½ cup **basmati rice**, rinsed

seeds from 4 **green cardamom pods**
    (*see page 14*)

2 tablespoons **sugar**

1 **PUT** the pistachio nuts and almonds in a heatproof bowl. Pour enough boiling water to cover over and let soak about 10 minutes. Drain the nuts, then use your fingers to pop them out of their skins before coarsely chopping them.

2 **COMBINE** the milk and rice in a saucepan over medium heat and simmer 12 minutes, stirring frequently so the grains do not stick on the bottom of the pan and the milk does not boil over.

3 **RESERVE** 1 teaspoon of the chopped nuts for garnishing and stir the rest of the nuts and the cardamom seeds into the rice. Simmer, stirring, 2 to 3 minutes while the milk and rice bubble gently.

4 **STIR** in the sugar and continue to simmer, stirring, 5 to 6 minutes until the sugar dissolves and the rice is tender.

5 **SPOON** into serving bowls or cups, sprinkle with the reserved chopped nuts, and serve at once. Alternatively, let the pudding cool completely, then transfer to a bowl, cover with plastic wrap, and refrigerate until required, up to 2 days. This pudding can be served chilled or at room temperature. It can be reheated once: place it in a saucepan and slowly heat 5 to 7 minutes until piping hot—add several tablespoons of milk to prevent it from becoming too thick.

MILK FUDGE *BARFI*

**MAKES 16 PIECES   PREPARATION TIME: 5 MINUTES, PLUS COOLING TIME
COOKING TIME: 12 MINUTES**

*This traditional Indian candy made from dried or condensed milk and cooked with
sugar until it solidifies can be flavored with nuts, flour, spices—and even lentils
or vegetables. The basic version here will get you started. For a spicy variation,
add a pinch of cardamom while mixing. Serve small squares of this fudge with
a cup of tea or coffee, or at the end of a meal.*

1 teaspoon **butter**

¼ cup **sugar**

¾ cup **heavy cream**

1 cup **whole milk powder**

1 MELT the butter in a heavy-bottomed saucepan over medium heat.
Add the sugar and cook, stirring continuously, 3 minutes, or until
the sugar melts.

2 ADD the cream and simmer, stirring occasionally, 3 minutes.

3 STIR in the milk powder and simmer, stirring, 5 minutes, or until
the mixture becomes stiff and begins to leave the side of the pan.

4 POUR the mixture onto a sheet of waxed paper and let it stand
a couple of minutes, then use a wet metal spatula to shape it into
a 4-inch square about ¾ inch thick.

5 LEAVE the mixture to cool completely. Using a sharp knife, cut
the cooled fudge into sixteen 1-inch squares. Serve with coffee or tea,
or transfer to an airtight container and refrigerate up to 5 days.

SEMOLINA PUDDING *SHEERA*

SERVES 4 PREPARATION TIME: 5 MINUTES COOKING TIME: 7 MINUTES

This dessert is served during religious festivals, such as Diwali, the Hindu festival of lights. A quick and simple comforting pudding, it can be prepared in just a few minutes, just before serving.

4 tablespoons **butter**

heaped ½ cup **fine semolina**

¼ cup **sugar**

¼ cup **heavy cream**

1 **banana**, sliced

6 shelled **pistachio nuts**, chopped

seeds from 2 **green cardamom pods**
   (*see page 14*)

1 **BRING** ¾ cup plus 2 tablespoons water to a boil. Melt the butter in a saucepan over medium heat. Add the semolina and cook 5 minutes, stirring constantly, or until the mixture becomes clumpy, light sand in color, and has a toasty aroma.

2 **POUR** the boiling water over, add the sugar and cream, and stir until the sugar dissolves.

3 **STIR** in the banana, pistachio nuts, and cardamom seeds. Serve warm.

CREAMY YOGURT DESSERT

SHRIKHAND

SERVES 4   PREPARATION TIME: 5 MINUTES, PLUS AT LEAST 8 HOURS DRAINING FOR THE YOGURT

Strained yogurt has a decadently rich and creamy texture—for the best results, use yogurt made from whole milk. This dish from western Indian often features fruits, nuts, and spices and is sometimes served alongside deep fried breads.

2¼ cups **plain yogurt**

seeds from 5 **green cardamom pods**
(*see page 14*)

2 tablespoons **powdered sugar**

6 **saffron strands**

15 **pistachio nuts**, shelled and crushed or chopped

1 PUT the yogurt in a large, fine-mesh nylon strainer and place it over a bowl. Cover and refrigerate at least 8 hours, or overnight, to allow the whey, or excess liquid, to drain away.

2 GRIND the cardamom seeds to a powder with a mortar and pestle.

3 PLACE the yogurt, ground cardamom seeds, sugar, and saffron strands in a bowl and mix well.

4 STIR in the nuts, cover the bowl with plastic wrap, and chill in the refrigerator until ready to serve. Serve with hot Pooris (see page 30).

MANGO YOGURT DRINK

AAM KA LASSI

SERVES 4   PREPARATION TIME: 5 MINUTES

Popular during the hot summer months, particularly in northern India, this refreshing beverage is made by blending yogurt and spices. Savory versions may be seasoned with cumin and black pepper, but this classic sweet variation uses mango pulp. The Alphonso mango, one of the sweetest in the world, yields the tastiest result. If fresh mangoes are not available, you can buy mango pulp in cans from many supermarkets and most Asian food stores.

seeds from 2 **green cardamom pods**
  (*see page 14*)

4 large ripe **mangoes**, peeled and chopped
  (*see page 18*)

2¼ cups **plain yogurt**

2¼ cups **milk**

4 teaspoons **sugar**

ice, to serve

1 GRIND the cardamom seeds to a powder with a pestle and mortar.

2 PUT the chopped mangoes in a blender and blend until a smooth pulp forms. This should yield about 2¼ cups mango pulp.

3 ADD the ground cardamom seeds, yogurt, milk and sugar to the blender and blend until smooth. Alternatively, whisk all the ingredients together in a large bowl.

4 SERVE at once, over ice, in tall glasses.

SPICY TEA *MASALA CHAI*

SERVES 4   PREPARATION TIME: 5 MINUTES   COOKING TIME: 10 MINUTES

Fragrant cinnamon, cardamom, clove, and fennel combine to create a delightfully spicy tea. In India, teas are defined by the regions in which they are grown, hence the names Darjeeling, Assam, and Nilgiri—so experiment with different varieties to find the one you like best.

2-inch piece **cassia bark** or **cinnamon stick**

2 **green cardamom pods**, lightly crushed

2 **cloves**

1 teaspoon **fennel seeds**

2 teaspoons **black tea leaves**

4 teaspoons **sugar** (optional)

1 cup **milk**

1 **BOIL** 2¼ cups water in a saucepan over high heat. Add the cassia bark or cinnamon, cardamom pods, cloves, and fennel seeds and continue boiling 2 minutes.

2 **ADD** the tea leaves and sugar, if using, then reduce the heat to low and simmer 1 minute.

3 **POUR** in the milk and continue simmering 2 minutes longer.

4 **STRAIN** the tea into teacups or mugs and serve at once.

PART 3

THE MENUS

*Indian meals are informal and **friendly** affairs where the guests (even unexpected ones) are **welcomed** with open arms. Unlike Western meals that are often divided into multiple **courses**, Indian meals consist of several dishes all served at once, with the main dish usually being a particularly **elaborate** preparation. The full spectrum of **flavors**, from cool, rich and mild to spicy, hot, pungent, and sweet, is also part of the **meal**. Rice or bread (or both) are indispensable staples.*

*This **relaxed** approach means the possibilities for combining appetizers, side dishes, condiments, and main dishes are nearly **limitless**. The menus here are only **guides** to what an Indian host or hostess might serve for specific occasions. Once you have selected one, make sure to read through the individual **recipes**, compile a shopping list, and then review the **easy-to-follow** timeline so that preparing your menu is as **peaceful** and stress-free as possible.*

*Once you have the hang of following the menus, feel free to **mix** and match some of your favorite recipes from this book to **create** new menus to share with your friends and **family**.*

SIMPLE LUNCH

TIME PLAN

This simple lunch suggestion offers all the flavors of India in one go. It is not too spicy for lunchtime but has all the components to make a balanced Indian meal with different colors and textures.

SWEET POTATO CURRY

(see page 75)

CHICKEN JALFREZI

(see page 96)

CARROT SALAD

(see page 163)

CILANTRO CHUTNEY

(see page 19)

PLAIN BASMATI RICE

(see page 31)

Halve all the recipe ingredients if you are preparing a meal for two people. The cilantro chutney and the paste for the chicken dish can be made the night before. The onions, garlic, and chilies for the chicken and the vegetables for the carrot salad can also be chopped and stored in an airtight container overnight.

PM
12.30   COOK the chicken dish, then set aside and let cool.

1.00   PEEL, chop, and boil the sweet potatoes; drain well and set aside.

1.15   SEASON the carrot salad ingredients while the potatoes are boiling, then set aside to serve at room temperature.

1.30   CHOP the chili for the sweet potato dish and fry it with the cumin seeds, then finish cooking the potato dish; cover and keep warm.

1.45   COOK the rice just before serving, so it will be piping hot.

1.50   REHEAT the chicken in the saucepan over medium-low heat. Quickly reheat the sweet potatoes as well, if necessary, while the chicken reheats.

2.00   SERVE the Sweet Potato Curry, Chicken Jalfrezi, and Plain Basmati Rice hot, with the Carrot Salad and Cilantro Chutney.

PREPARATION NOTES

Save time by using **CHILI POWDER** instead of green chilies for the chicken dish, if you like. The difference in flavor will be subtle, and the final result will be just as delicious.

LUNCH BOX

TANDOORI CHICKEN BITES

(see page 51)

CUMIN-INFUSED PEAS

(see page 148)

SPICED RICE

(see page 32)

MANGO CHUTNEY

(see page 19)

TIME PLAN

All the dishes in this menu can be prepared the day before and make an enjoyable change from cold sushi or sandwiches. The menu avoids sauce-based dishes, so there is no danger of spills in your bag.

All these recipes serve four, so you will need to adjust the quantities to meet your needs: halve the recipes if preparing only two lunch boxes or quarter them if you are preparing only one. The day or evening before, marinate and roast or broil the chicken bites, then let them cool completely and refrigerate, covered, overnight. Also make the pea dish the night before and store in a sealed container once it is cool. The rice dish is best made fresh in the morning, but you can also make it the night before if you prefer. The chutney can be prepared a few days in advance and stored in the refrigerator.

AM 7.15 COOK the rice and let cool. Make sure it is completely cool before you pack it for transporting.

7.50 PACK the Tandoori Chicken Bites, the Cumin-Infused Peas, and the Spiced Rice in one container and the Mango Chutney in a separate sealed container.

PREPARATION NOTES

For extra flavor sprinkle some **CILANTRO LEAVES** over the chicken, rice, and peas before packing them. You can **TRANSFORM** leftover Tandoori Chicken Bites into Chicken Tikka Masala (see page 84) for an evening meal and store any leftover mango chutney in the refrigerator—it keeps up to 2 weeks.

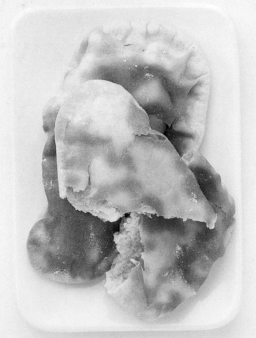

MIDWEEK LUNCH WITH FAMILY

TIME PLAN

Simple and mild dishes with a hint of chili heat and spice make up this quick and easy lunch menu for four. The chicken dish doesn't contain too much spice and is softened by the coconut and nuts in the sauce. It is like having take-out from your favorite Indian restaurant, only nicer. The lentils provide a balance to the creamy chicken—a hearty recipe for all the family.

TOMATO, ONION, AND CHILI SALAD

(see page 160)

CREAMY CHICKEN CURRY

(see page 99)

TEMPERED RED LENTILS

(see page 143)

NAANS

(see page 26)

Boil the red lentils the night before until they become mushy, but don't add the spices for the tempering. The naans can also be made ahead and then reheated before serving, but in Indian households they are always made fresh.

AM 11.00 MAKE and knead the naan dough, then cover the bowl and set aside in a warm place to rise.

PM 12.00 COOK the chicken curry, but do not add the ginger or garam masala, then set aside to cool completely.

12.30 MAKE the salad, then cover and chill.

12.45 PREHEAT the oven to 400°F and grease a baking sheet.

12.50 SHAPE and bake the naans. Wrap them in a clean dish towel to keep warm if they are finished baking before the other dishes are reheated.

1:15 REHEAT the chicken curry, stirring in the ginger and garam masala.

1:25 REHEAT the lentils and fry the curry leaves and other spices for tempering, then stir the buttery spice mixture into the lentils and finish cooking.

1:30 SERVE the Creamy Chicken Curry, Tempered Red Lentils, and Naans hot, with the chilled Tomato, Onion, and Chili Salad.

PREPARATION NOTES

For **VARIETY** use split yellow lentils instead of red. The exact cooking time depends on how old they are—older lentils take longer. If the **SAUCE** seems dry when reheating the chicken, stir in some water and watch carefully so it does not burn.

MIDWEEK LUNCH WITH FRIENDS

SPICED WHITE FISH COOKED IN COCONUT

(see page 127)

SPICED BLACK-EYED PEAS

(see page 144)

FENUGREEK FLATBREADS

(see page 28)

SEMOLINA PUDDING

(see page 180)

PREPARATION NOTES

FRESH FISH should smell like the sea—not "fishy." The eyes should be clear and the gills bright red when purchased. In southern India, this fish dish is traditionally made with seer fish, a type of **MACKEREL**. So, if you prefer, you can replace the sole specified in the recipe with mackerel.

TIME PLAN

The fresh flavors of the southern Indian-style fish dish in this menu complement the nuttiness of the black-eyed peas and the fenugreek-spiced flatbreads. The semolina pudding is a gorgeous comfort dessert that is reassuringly filling and satisfying.

All of the recipes in this menu are so quick and simple, they can be made on the day of the lunch, before your friends arrive.

12.00 PM **MAKE** the semolina pudding. Leave it to cool completely and then cover and set aside.

12.35 **POUR** boiling water over the tamarind pulp in the fish recipe to extract the seeds and fibers. Mix the tamarind juice with the spices and boiling water in the recipe and set aside.

12.45 **COOK** the spiced peas but do not add the ginger and cilantro leaves at the end of the recipe; set aside.

1.00 **MIX** and knead the dough for the flatbreads, then cover the bowl and let rest.

1.15 **COOK** the spiced fish dish and keep it warm over low heat, without boiling.

1.25 **REHEAT** the spiced peas until hot, then sprinkle them with the ginger and cilantro; cover and keep them warm.

1.30 **SHAPE** and cook the flatbreads just before serving.

1.45 **SERVE** the Spiced White Fish Cooked in Coconut, Spiced Black-Eyed Peas, and Fenugreek Flatbreads hot.

2.15 **REHEAT** the Semolina Pudding. If it has become too thick, add ¼ cup water and stir until smooth and heated through. Sprinkle with the nuts and serve warm.

WEEKEND LUNCH WITH FAMILY

TIME PLAN

Using mostly humble ingredients, this relaxing, well-deserved weekend menu features the robust, warming flavors of northern Indian cuisine. It is an ideal, comforting choice after a long week.

CHICKEN TIKKA MASALA
(see page 84)

BUTTERY SPINACH AND POTATOES
(see page 71)

PULAO RICE WITH PEAS
(see page 32)

CARDAMOM ICE CREAM
(see page 175)

Marinate the Tandoori Chicken Bites (see page 51) for the chicken recipe the evening before or the morning of the lunch. The ice cream is a handy, standby dessert to have in the freezer, as it can be made up to three months in advance. If you want to get even more of a head start, cook the rice in the morning and reheat it just before serving.

AM 11.55 **CUT** the potatoes and rinse the spinach, then prepare the remaining ingredients for the spinach and potato recipe and set aside.

PM 12.15 **ASSEMBLE** the ingredients for the chicken dish and set aside. Rinse the rice, assemble the spices it is cooked with it, chop the chili, and then set aside.

1.00 **COOK** the chicken dish, then set aside for reheating just before serving. Preheat the oven to 325°F.

1.15 **COOK** the spinach and potatoes and keep them warm, covered with foil, in the oven until ready to serve.

1.55 **COOK** the rice with the peas, then cover and keep hot.

2.10 **REHEAT** the chicken dish over medium-low heat, stirring occasionally, 7 to 9 minutes until hot, but not boiling.

2.20 **SERVE** the Chicken Tikka Masala, Buttery Spinach and Potatoes, and Pulao Rice with Peas hot.

2.40 **TRANSFER** the ice cream to the refrigerator to soften.

2.55 **SCOOP** the Cardamom Ice Cream into bowls and serve.

PREPARATION NOTES

Indian **ICE CREAM** is denser than Western ice creams, so remember to take it out of the freezer so it can soften in time. For an authentic touch, freeze the ice cream in **TRADITIONAL** conical-shaped molds sold in Indian food stores.

WEEKEND LUNCH WITH FRIENDS

PREPARATION NOTES

The **LENTIL** dish is best eaten the day it is made, so don't prepare it the evening before. The spices are most flavorful when added just before serving.

TIME PLAN

Just a few striking ingredients make up this simple yet exotic menu, which offers maximum flavor with minimum effort or skill. The earthiness of the Plain Basmati Rice compliments the aromatic dishes of this delicious spread.

A day or two before, make the cashew nut dessert, transfer it to an airtight container, and refrigerate. Make the lentils in the morning but don't add the spices. The shrimp curry is best cooked at the last minute, but if you are worried about time, it can be made in the morning and reheated with an extra ¼ cup water stirred in.

12.00 PM **PREPARE** and assemble all the ingredients for the shrimp curry and set aside. Rinse the rice and set aside.

12.40 **PREHEAT** the oven to 325°F. Cook the cabbage dish until the cabbage is just tender, then transfer to an ovenproof serving dish, cover with foil, and leave in the oven until ready to serve. Take care not to overcook the cabbage.

12.55 **PREPARE** and cook the lentils, until the point where you add the boiling water, then set aside for reheating just before serving.

1.00 **MAKE** the shrimp curry and keep it warm.

1.20 **COOK** the rice. Reheat the lentils, mashing them against the side of the pan, then let simmer while the rice cooks.

1.30 **SERVE** the Cabbage with Red Chilies, Malabar Shrimp Curry, Maharashtrian Lentils, and Plain Basmati Rice hot in separate serving dishes in the middle of the table for everyone to help themselves.

2.15 **ARRANGE** the Cashew Nut Diamonds on a plate (as you would a plate of cookies) and invite your guests to nibble on them while they drink tea, coffee, or dessert wine.

SIMPLE DINNER

TIME PLAN

The contrasting colors and diversity of flavors in these dishes make a simple yet delightful meal. The creamy and comforting chicken combined with the lightly spiced greens, tangy tomato relish, and turmeric-infused rice make this an all-around pleaser.

BUTTER CHICKEN
(see page 88)

SPICED GREENS
(see page 156)

TURMERIC RICE
(see page 33)

TOMATO CHUTNEY
(see page 21)

Halve all the recipe ingredients if you are preparing dinner for two. Marinate the chicken the night before, then cover and place it in the refrigerator. The chutney can be made any time up to two weeks in advance and stored in a sealed jar.

PM

6.45 PREPARE the ingredients for the Butter Chicken sauce, stopping after step 4. Remove the pan from the heat and set aside.

7.00 PREPARE all the ingredients for the Spiced Greens dish. Rinse the rice and set aside. Remove the chicken pieces from the refrigerator.

7.30 FRY the spices for the rice, then complete the recipe.

7.40 REHEAT the sauce for the chicken over medium heat, then reduce the heat to low. Add the butter and chicken pieces to the sauce and simmer until the chicken is cooked through.

7.50 FRY the greens.

8.00 SERVE the Butter Chicken, Spiced Greens, and Turmeric Rice hot. Put the Tomato Chutney in a small, nonmetallic dish or ramekin and serve.

PREPARATION NOTES

Use **KALE** or **SWISS CHARD** in the Spiced Greens for variety. It is best to buy the greens on the day or the day before, no earlier. Choose greens with firm, uniform-colored leaves that are not wilted or discolored. Rinse them thoroughly before cooking to remove the sandy grit.

ROMANTIC DINNER

HALIBUT WITH GREEN CHILIES AND CILANTRO

(see page 123)

GREEN PEPPERS WITH CUMIN

(see page 152)

SAFFRON RICE

(see page 33)

EXOTIC FRUIT SALAD

(see page 172)

PREPARATION NOTES

HALIBUT is a large, mild, white flatfish and is available in steaks or filets. The firm, meaty flesh has a subtle flavor and complements sauces wonderfully. If you want to **SAVE TIME**, the fruit salad can be made up to two days ahead of the dinner, but the flavors really are best when it is made fresh.

TIME PLAN

This menu balances a number of lively flavors, striking colors, tantalizing textures, and fragrant aromas to create a memorable dining experience.

To prepare this meal for two people, halve all the recipe quantities. Make the cilantro paste in step 3 of the halibut recipe the night before the dinner, then refrigerate in an airtight container until ready to use.

PM
6.45 PREPARE the ingredients for the green pepper dish and set aside. Rinse the rice and set aside. Soak the tamarind pulp and prepare the remaining ingredients for the halibut dish.

7.10 CHOP the papaya and mango for the salad, then slice the banana and hull the strawberries. Place all the fruit in a serving bowl and add the lime juice and sugar, then cover and refrigerate.

7.25 SOAK the saffron strands and fry the spices for the rice dish, then continue with the recipe, cooking the rice until it is fluffy.

7.35 MAKE the halibut dish, while the rice is cooking. Be careful not to break up the fish pieces.

7.45 FRY the garlic and onion for the green pepper dish, then complete the dish while the halibut is cooking.

7.55 REMOVE the fruit salad from the refrigerator.

8.00 SERVE the Halibut with Green Chilies and Cilantro, Green Peppers with Cumin, and Saffron Rice hot, followed by the Exotic Fruit Salad at room temperature.

MIDWEEK DINNER WITH FAMILY

GRIDDLED CHICKEN

(see page 95)

MIXED VEGETABLE CURRY

(see page 76)

KIDNEY BEANS IN SPICY TOMATO AND GARLIC SAUCE

(see page 67)

BALTI POTATOES

(see page 139)

EXOTIC LEAVENED NAANS

(see page 27)

PREPARATION NOTES

If any vegetable in the curry isn't to your family's liking, try substituting it with **GREEN BEANS** or **ZUCCHINI**. Add them along with the broccoli and red pepper to ensure they are tender before adding them to the masala.

From the quick, flash-fry chicken dish to the warming kidney bean curry and the freshness of the herbs in the mixed vegetables, this relaxed, informal menu is a perfect treat for a family with a hectic schedule. The recipes are not too chili-hot, so everyone will enjoy them.

Make the naans the night before and store in an airtight container. Cook the kidney bean dish as well so the flavors have time to develop, but do not add the final seasoning of salt and garam masala or the cilantro leaves. You can also make the masala paste for the vegetable curry and store it in the refrigerator.

PM

5.50   PEEL, chop, and boil the potatoes for the balti dish. Make the coarse paste that flavors the dish while the potatoes are boiling.

6.05   FINISH cooking the potato dish, then set aside in the pan.

6.35   COOK the vegetable curry, using the masala paste prepared the night before. Set aside in the pan, ready for reheating.

7.00   PREPARE the Griddled Chicken, cooking until just before the fresh fenugreek leaves are added. Cover and set aside until serving. Preheat the oven to 350°F.

7.40   REHEAT the kidney beans until hot. Stir in the salt and garam masala, transfer to a serving bowl, and sprinkle with cilantro leaves. While the beans are heating, finish the chicken dish and keep it hot in the oven.

7.45   SPRINKLE the naans with a little water, wrap in foil, and put in the oven to reheat.

7.55   REHEAT the potatoes.

8.00   SERVE the Griddled Chicken, Mixed Vegetable Curry, Kidney Beans in Spicy Tomato and Garlic Gravy, Balti Potatoes, and Exotic Leavened Naans hot.

MIDWEEK DINNER WITH FRIENDS

TIME PLAN

The various fresh herbs, whole spices, and spice blends used in these recipes make this an unforgettable meal to savor. The refreshing, spiced fresh tomato soup seasons the palate for the dishes to follow, which combines North Indian cooking with Goanese tastes and aromas.

The day before, marinate the pork for the vindaloo dish and make the soup, then store everything in the refrigerator. Leave the yogurt for the dessert to strain overnight.

PM

6.00 PREPARE all the ingredients for the green bean dish and the chickpea curry and set aside. There are a lot of ingredients, so make sure you have everything ready before you start cooking.

6.15 FINISH preparing the yogurt dessert, then cover and refrigerate.

6.20 REMOVE the marinated pork from the refrigerator. Rinse the basmati rice and set aside.

6.25 COOK the green bean recipe until the beans are not quite tender, then set aside in the same pan for reheating.

6.40 TRANSFER the marinated pork to a saucepan and finish cooking.

6.55 BREW the tea for the chickpeas, finish the recipe, and set aside.

7.30 COOK the rice. Just before the rice finishes cooking, quickly reheat the green beans over high heat, stirring. At the same time, reheat the chickpea curry over medium-high heat until hot.

7.45 REMOVE the soup from the refrigerator, put it in a saucepan, and reheat, then ladle into bowls. Serve the soup as a separate first course, or Indian-style along with the other dishes.

7.55 TRANSFER the rice to a large serving bowl.

8.00 SERVE the Tomato Soup, Pork Vindaloo, Chickpea Curry, Green Beans with Garlic and Mustard Seeds, and Plain Basmati Rice hot.

8.45 SERVE the chilled Creamy Yogurt Dessert.

DINNER PARTY

TIME PLAN

This stunning dinner party lineup takes you and your guests on a tasting tour of India. Spicy, mild, sweet, and pungent flavors all abound, and although the menu might look elaborate, many of the dishes can be prepared the day before—so you get to enjoy the party, too.

To serve eight people, double all the recipes. The day before, cook the chicken dish, the basmati rice for the biryani, and the prawn mixture for the pooris, then make the dessert. Refrigerate overnight.

PM

2.30 MAKE the garam masala and prepare the remaining ingredients for the biryani. Prepare the ingredients for the paneer and fish dishes.

2.50 COOK the lamb for the biryani and let cool.

3.00 MAKE the dough for the pooris, then knead, shape, roll out, and fry.

4.00 COOK the fish curry, then let cool completely, cover, and chill.

4.30 COOK the paneer dish, but do not add the ginger, cream, garam masala, or coriander, then set aside to cool.

5.30 ASSEMBLE the layers of lamb and rice for the biryani. Cover the casserole and put in the refrigerator until required.

7.00 PREHEAT the oven to 350°F for cooking the biryani and reheating the pooris. Remove the biryani from the refrigerator.

7.25 PUT the biryani in the oven.

7.45 REHEAT the shrimp mixture, the fish curry, and the chicken in separate pans over low heat, stirring occasionally, then cover tightly.

7.50 REHEAT the pooris in the oven while the biryani finishes cooking.

7.55 ASSEMBLE the Shrimp Pooris and remove the biryani from the oven. Reheat the paneer, then stir in the ginger and cream and sprinkle with garam masala and cilantro.

8.00 SERVE the Shrimp Pooris hot, as a first course, then serve the other hot dishes together and round off the meal with the Coconut Treats.

COCKTAIL PARTY

ONION FRITTERS
(see page 39)

VEGETABLE SAMOSAS
(see page 36)

DEEP-FRIED FISH
(see page 56)

SHRIMP FRITTERS
(see page 59)

LAMB KEBABS
(see page 55)

A SELECTION OF CHUTNEYS AND RELISHES, INCLUDING MINT AND YOGURT CHUTNEY *(see page 19)*, COCONUT AND TOMATO CHUTNEY *(see page 20)*, AND CUCUMBER RELISH
(see page 22)

TIME PLAN

Fantastic flavors for all tastes make up this cocktail party menu. These dishes—generous bite-size portions of popular appetizers—are more than just nibbles. Arrange small portions of each item on serving plates and refill as needed. This menu caters for six to eight guests.

The night before, marinate the ground lamb for the kebabs, then mold the meat around the metal skewers, cover, and refrigerate. Make and assemble the samosas, then cover and refrigerate. The chutneys and relishes should also be made the day before.

PM

5.15 MAKE the batter mixtures for the Onion Fritters, Deep-fried Fish, and Shrimp Fritters. Cover and set each aside in a separate bowl.

6.10 PREHEAT the broiler to medium. Remove the samosas and fish from the refrigerator. Preheat the oven to 325°F.

6.15 GRILL the lamb kebabs, then wrap in foil and place in the oven.

6.30 HEAT the oil for deep-frying the samosas to 375°F.

6.35 DEEP-FRY the samosas in batches, then drain on paper towels. When they are all fried, wrap them in foil and keep them warm in the oven. Reheat the oil and deep-fry the onion fritters, then put them in the oven to keep warm.

7.00 PUT a fresh batch of oil in the fryer and reheat to 375°F. Fry the shrimp fritters and drain on paper towels.

7.15 REMOVE everything from the oven and arrange on serving plates.

7.30 SERVE all the appetizers hot, with the chilled chutneys and relishes, buffet style for your guests to help themselves, or arrange small portions of each item on serving plates, as shown, then pass them around and refill the plates as needed.

INDEX